HELP!

MY EXTRAORDINARY PURPOSE iS SiMMERING iN A POT OF PREPARATION STEW

*10 Ingredients to Prepare for An
Extraordinary Purpose*

IEASHA T. EDWARDS, MPH

DEDICATION

This book is dedicated to the readers who choose to make sense out of life even when it doesn't and when life takes you on a wild ride, testing your core beliefs, you wouldn't think twice about using food metaphors like "potluck" (Chapter 4) to get a laugh out of it. I am your person and you are mine!

Thanks to my mom for teaching me that being different is an advantage and God can use the most unlikely of people. My life's purpose has been shaped most by this principle. Mom, you are my hero.

"Every one of us who embraces the Glory of God as our purpose will end up doing great things precisely because we do God-things. His holy hand resting on the least act renders the ordinary extraordinary."

—Beth Moore, author, Esther: It's Tough Being a Woman

CONTENTS

Prologue.. viii

Introduction xi
Basic Assumptions about Yourself and Your Life........................... xii

Chapter 1 Purpose.. 1
Pot of Preparation 1
God's Kingdom Purpose.. 2
God's Purpose for Mankind... 10
Finding My Place in the Kingdom of God.................................... 13
Pot of Preparation Stew Reflection... 14
Prayer for Unlocking God's Promises.. 16

Chapter 2 Patience 17
Crock-Pot® 17
Fruit of the Spirit Check: Patience 17
Seasons of Preparation 19
Identifying the Timing of Your Assignment................................. 22
Crock-Pot® Reflection 24
Prayer for Endurance 25

Chapter 3 Pressure 26
Pot Timer 26
Fruit of the Spirit Check: Peace... 27
Principles Governing God's Timing... 27
Reigning in God's Timing.. 29
Pot Timer Reflections 31
Prayer for Peace... 32

Chapter 4   Pursue.. 33

Potluck.. 33

Fruit of the Spirit Check: Gentleness (Kindness).............. 34

Making the Best of Hodgepodge Experiences.................. 34

Change Course in Pursuit of Greater Purpose................. 36

Potluck Reflections 38

Prayer for Kingdom Purpose.. 38

Chapter 5   Potter's Wheel 40

Position... 40

Fruit of the Spirit Check: Joy 41

Discovering Purpose 41

Date with Destiny.. 42

Potter's Wheel Reflections 44

Fruit of the Spirit Check: Joy 45

Confession for Joy-Filled Purpose 46

Chapter 6   Pot Belly 47

Ponder 47

Fruit of the Spirit Check: Faithfulness 48

Pot Belly Reflections 51

Fruit of the Spirit Check: Faithfulness 51

Prayer for Faith Perspective 52

Chapter 7   Pothole... 53

Purge 53

Fruit of the Spirit Check: Love....................................... 53

Pothole Reflections 61

Declaration for Embracing God's Love 62

Chapter 8   Purify 63

Potter's Kiln 63

Fruit of the Spirit Check: Self-Control 64

Potter's Kiln Reflections... 71

Walk in Purpose Check 71

Prayer for Revealing My Life Hidden in Christ................ 71

Chapter 9   Present 73

Pot 'o' Gold 73

Fruit of the Spirit Check: Goodness 74

Cultivating Goodness 74

Authentic Alpha Womanhood 75

Alpha Women and Integrity 77

Pot 'o' Gold Reflections 79

Fruit of the Spirit Check: Goodness 79

Assessment for Discovering My Alpha Mechanics 80

Chapter 10 Present 81

Vessel of Honor 81

Fruit of the Spirit Check: Kindness 82

Vessel of Honor Reflections 86

Fruit of the Spirit: Kindness 87

Potter's Refinement Project 87

Bonus Chapter 89

Purposefully Single and Preparing 89

Follow Ruth's Way 91

Alpha Women and Dating 96

Case Study: We're Getting Married 99

The Challenge 101

God: My First Love 102

Confession for the Purposefully Single Woman 103

PROLOGUE

I usually visited Rachel's room last. This night I found her frenzied—number flash cards strewn about, colored blocks organized by shape, and pages of alphabet trace "thingies" on the floor.

"Fifty, fifty-one, fifty-two," Rachel frantically recited as I peered over her shoulder to see exactly what all the fuss was.

"Please, please go over these with me. Will you?" Rachel's plea pulled at my heartstrings.

"Sure," I said, though I wasn't quite sure to which Kindergarten classroom Rachel would lead me. Alphabet City, I suspected, but I was plain unwilling to count numbers Sesame Street-style. I couldn't do it anymore. I hadn't done this in so many years, and trying to remember how to do it now didn't thrill me. Don't get me wrong; sing-song methods of learning reign supreme. It's just that it was more than thirty minutes past bedtime, and even I began to feel the weight of my eyes overtake me. I wished Rachel would, instead, begin counting sheep.

One drill after the other, Rachel responded with the accuracy of a well-versed politician during a press conference. You'd think she was preparing for college finals, but no, it was kindergarten. Addition was the hot-topic agenda item.

"Five plus two is seven. If you take seven, which is five plus two, and then add one to it, it'll equal eight. That is correct, isn't it, Ieasha?" Gliding wooden abacus beads left to right, skimming rows for accuracy, she frequently backtracked, often appearing to challenge the very logic she used to derive her answer. "I still do not know how I'll remember this for tomorrow. If I don't pass, my life is over!"

My five-year-old's life is over? Upon seeing Rachel's apparent meltdown, I first thought, this girl cannot be serious. She was serious, in fact so serious, it concerned me. I had to intervene.

"You're not serious, are you? I mean, sweetie, close your eyes and think about what you'd like to be when you grow up. You got it?"

"Yeah, I want to be like my mom, a writer, like for TV or something like that."

"Good! So now, think about this. God already knew, even before you were born, that you'd want to be a writer or anything else you decided. He also knows that you must do well, first in kindergarten, then elementary school, and that it will not be until you do well in high school, graduate, and eventually go on to college that you will become a writer. God knows this." I had to come up with something. Okay?

At this point, Rachel looked intently into my eyes and then away, as if to analyse the validity of my message. Then she said it; her words were a much-needed distraction from these scholastic intensives.

"You know about God?" Rachel queried, at first in disbelief.

"Yes, and God wants the very best for you." I affirmed her and was glad to have made a connection. "He has a great plan for your life, so don't worry about tomorrow; the peace of God will be with you."

With the innocence of a five-year-old, she probed further, "Are you Jewish?"

"Jewish, well, no. Why do you ask?"

"Well, because you said God and peace of God!" What could I say about this five-year-old logic?

I did not bother going through explaining that other people know God, those of different nationalities and those from different countries. After all, her conclusion was not based on race or differences at all, but rather knowing who God is. Besides, this time, with the persistence of a car salesperson, Rachel's discovery—albeit only partially incorrect—revealed a rather convincing argument.

"C'mon. You're Jewish! I knew it! I'm Jewish and know about God, and so do you, so that makes you Jewish too!" Honestly, I would have been willing to become almost anything Rachel wanted at that hour. It was late, and as usual, she was convinced. Rachel was always convinced.

Readers of this book will profit from shared wisdom found in each chapter, if, with the same tenacity of a five-year-old, you ascribe to the belief that familiar experiences between women often connect us in an uncommon way. Discovering how each of your experiences "blend" collectively as essential ingredients in your pot of preparation stew is uncommon. Like Rachel, being convinced, you may not always make an immediate connection in your everyday walk in purpose, but be sure to look for the link anyway. A connection is there and begs to be revealed, one step at a time.

INTRODUCTION

Hello There, Woman of Purpose!

You, just like other women I know, live to experience a life chock-full of purpose. Right? Beyond this experience, you'll certainly want to realize your extraordinary life purpose, even if you're not exactly sure what your purpose is; how to access it, and that you're promised it—a promise that is backed by God before the beginning of time. Starting with God's plan for reconciliation, the extraordinary purpose is factored in God's plan for every believer. Women will learn the ingredients to overcoming setbacks while forging ahead, by first acknowledging:

1. Her walk in extraordinary purpose is predestined, waiting for her to discover it.
2. God's sovereign placement of gifts and talents in her for building up the kingdom of God.
3. Her current position in life works as part of God's perfect will.
4. Through atonement, God dispenses grace to cover human error and shortcomings.
5. Extraordinary purpose requires self-examination and cultivating "fruit of the spirit."

Who Is This Book For?

Help! My Extraordinary Purpose Is Simmering in a Pot of Preparation Stew will guide women readers in humor, truth, and bible-supported, practical life application—through the steps they must take to pursue the big "it" called purpose.

Detailing the immense preparation that is required from a woman to navigate life's "pothole" experiences, the book will provide her the tools to help her not only enjoy her journey but also capitalize on the "pot o' gold" (greatness) that begs to be released from within her. The joy she will experience as she "walks in purpose" and the inevitable respect for the process that is garnered as she learns, preparing for purpose, is just as integral to her destiny as the journey toward destiny itself.

BASIC ASSUMPTIONS ABOUT YOURSELF AND YOUR LIFE

There are a few things that I presume are basic characteristics of those reading this book. These qualities and traits may not be all-inclusive or pertain to all readers. If these traits do not describe you, it is equally important and maybe even more important that you take advantage of the material written in this book.

Much like the assumptions of faith, I believe there are some basic beliefs the readers of this book possess. Again, the list below is not all-inclusive and does not necessarily pertain to all readers. This book is meant to bring growth and encourage the reader to move beyond the place of destiny she is in now, to achieve the highest level of excellence God has ordained for her.

You Acknowledge:

1. Life on earth has a predestined purpose, and you are willing to discover the tools that serve to unlock God's plan for you in His kingdom and discover and operate in the factors that strengthen your destiny walk.
2. God's sovereignty places gifts, talents, and callings within believers as He chooses for His glory, for the building up of His kingdom and other collective purposes in the body of Christ.
3. God's perfect will for our lives includes supernatural protection but not a perfect, problem-free life. "In life you shall have tribulations,

be of good cheer; I have overcome the world" (John 16:33). Your destiny walk will not be perfect. Obedience counts, not perfection.

4. God's immense, unconditional love and compassion for you dispenses grace to cover mistakes, shortcomings, and "missing the mark." Through repentance, He restores you to right standing with Him so that you will have full access to His promises.

5. Pursuing purpose requires continual self-examination and exploration of ways to make improvements in your attitude, behaviors, and growth in your spiritual life. A primary goal should be developing the "fruit of the Spirit." (Find all of them listed in Galatians 5:22–23.)

How to Use This Book

God's plan for my life is directional; His plan for my life is sure! Ten chapters form a "pot" theme, including "Pot of Preparation," "Crock Pot," "Pothole," "Potter's Kiln," and "Vessel of Honor." Introductory text outlines in detail God's plan of reconciliation and how this links His purpose for all mankind. Closing text will "commission" readers not only as extraordinary purpose seekers but also as vessels of honor—honorary carriers of God's will for His kingdom.

Book Chapter Elements Include:

- End-of-chapter themed chapter reflections
- It's Your Turn devotionals
- Prayers/declarations aligning chapter themes, and
- Fruit of the Spirit Check self-assessments

Chapters 1 and 2 will transition the reader from academic knowing about purpose to developing the skills to move swiftly through each God-ordained assignment. Chapter 3 uncovers key attributes of each stage of preparation to help her maximize opportunities to cultivate character and integrity, reflecting God's intent for her, while turning away from personal beliefs and actions that can hinder her walk in purpose. How will she know when she has arrived in a "season of preparation"? Ingredients are found here.

By chapter 4, women not only know they should expect to pursue a life full of purpose but also have some pointers and tools to unlock their purposes. Presented with practical examples, women now must develop their thick skin for overcoming a mix of good and challenging experiences and the know-how to persevere despite obstacles before them. Being positioned on the potter's wheel does not feel good all the time. After all, just like a clay pot, women must undergo shaping, firing, and remaking to become the vessel of honor God intended. Chapters 5 and 6 mark the middle of the book, and just like everyday life, a woman will surely get stuck somewhere in the middle of her walk in purpose, asking "How much longer will it take?" The fruit of faithfulness will be her portion as she discovers greatness has gone before to prepare the way.

Chapters 7 and 8 personify what happens after learning the inherent value of life's pothole experiences and enduring the heat of the proverbial potter's kiln—supernatural healing for a wounded heart. "What more will I have to endure?" Women will yell "ouch!" time and again as they run head-on into life's character-building experiences, acquiring skills to overcome hurt from rejection and insult while cultivating the fruit of love. True purpose seekers will discover what is authentic and pure, gracefully embracing the fruit of self-control to persevere through the process.

Chapter 9, "Pot o' Gold," is not talking leprechauns and rainbows but the reward we get from cultivating the fruit of goodness, the product of authentic womanhood, integrity, and strength. What more can we expect and earnestly desire than going for the grand prize, the pot of gold? But wait! There's more goodness in store for those who stay the course. Finally, chapter 10 presents purposeful women who yield to preparation as a vessel of honor, not because your journey is perfect and without detours, but rather, because you stayed the course!

CHAPTER 1

PURPOSE

POT OF PREPARATION

Purposeful Women …
Celebrate Their Contribution to God's Kingdom Agenda
It Started Before the Beginning

Let's start with the basics. God's plan for your lives came together before the beginning of time. That's right! Your destiny was predetermined even before God created heaven and earth. It was decided before the birds and the bees became a legendary motif for explaining away procreation activities. It was decided long before the great debate over which came first, the chicken or the egg and long before Adam, Eve, and the infamous "apple" in the garden of Eden ever took place. The road to destiny was the narrow path set for you to travel before roads cleared the way through forests, before trees, before land, and before seas were ever created.

> [A Prayer of Moses the man of God.] Lord, thou hast been
> our dwelling place in all generations, Before the mountains
> were brought forth, or ever thou hadst formed the earth

and the world, even from everlasting to everlasting, thou [art] God. (Psalm 90:1–2)

Who verily was foreordained before the foundation of the world, but was manifest in these last times for you. (1 Peter 1:20)

Destiny actually awaited your arrival! Imagine that. God preordained your arrival and marked your placement in His kingdom. All pieces of the destiny puzzle fit together perfectly. There was never a time when God had to refer to another model to draw inspiration or figure out where each piece should fit. By design, God created the mold and fashioned each well-constructed piece Himself, giving each of us a specific purpose or dedicated plan within His kingdom.

For [the children] being not yet born, neither having done any good or evil that the purpose of God according to election might stand, not of works, but of him that calleth. (Romans 9:11)

GOD'S KINGDOM PURPOSE

What is the purpose of God? How do you discover His plan? The purpose of God is clearly defined in scripture and has its root in the overall plan for humanity:

Purpose, of God: (Plan of God): pur'-pus : The word "purpose" seems to be an equivalent of the word "decree" as used in regard to man's relation to eternity. More correctly stated, it softens the word "decree" and refers back to the cause of the decree as lodged in an intelligent design and forward to an aim consistent with the character of God.

("Purpose, of God." International Standard Bible Encyclopedia. Edited by James Orr. Blue Letter Bible, 1913. April 1, 2007, March 17, 2010.)

Seek Purpose. Whether you realize it or not, the longings you have in your heart to identify your purpose for living were placed there by God. Seeking our God-ordained purpose is not only normal but also as divine as His promises are sure: "And ye shall seek me, and find [me], when ye shall search for me with all your heart" (Jeremiah 29:13). We seek so much from God already; He actually delights in this.

You also ask many questions about your purpose. Why am I here on earth? What is my life's calling? The questions, for which you seek answers, align with your individual purposes in His kingdom. However, that's not all. The purpose of God declares plainly in scripture His position as sovereign Creator, the establisher of your collective, corporate kingdom purpose and unique, individual purposes for all humanity. Plainly stated in scripture are three core features of God's purpose for humanity:

1. Make disciples and preach the gospel (Matthew 28:18–20)
2. Oversee the ministry of reconciliation (2 Corinthians 5:18)
3. Perform works for the sake of the gospel (1 Peter 4:10–11)

Now, it's not difficult to believe that the will of God directly links to His purpose for creating humankind in the first place. By establishing this foundational truth, you can now pursue God's plan for your life with surety.

> In whom also we have obtained an inheritance, being predestinated according to the purpose of him who worketh all things after the counsel of his own will: that we should be to the praise of his glory, who first trusted in Christ. (Ephesians 1:11)

Five keys we learn about God's purpose for you from the scripture above:

1. You have access to God's inheritance through Jesus.
2. God established your inheritance before the beginning of time.
3. Purpose in God was the plan for your life.
4. God looked to His own will for guidance in creating your purpose.
5. Humankind's overall purpose is to bring God glory, which happens as we fulfill the will of God.

Added to the above verse, we can see a common thread throughout scripture: "Preordained before the beginning of time, God established purpose for those whom He calls His sons" (Romans 8:14, 29). The reference to "sons" is gender neutral, referring to both women and men. Through Jesus, the Christ, "sonship" is each believer's inherent birthright, regardless of gender, race, or background. We all possess "the blessing" as Jesus did. These include: royal priest, king, lord, high priest, and chief apostle (Matthew 21:11, Zachariah 6:13, Psalm 24:8).

Positioned by the Will of God

What is the will of God? Positioned within God's purpose is "the mystery of His will," which He makes known to believers, "according to His good pleasure which He hath purposed in Himself" (Ephesians 1:9). That's fantastic! God's purpose is to reveal to us His will for our life, and He is very delighted to do this. Successful navigation in the kingdom of God requires that you become knowledgeable of His will. He takes a unique approach in unveiling the manner in which He chooses to reveal His will. Just as policies, decrees, and edicts govern successful kingdom operations likewise, God's kingdom flourishes as the people of God follow the plan God has for His kingdom.

God's Kingdom Operations

The kingdom of God works as a highly structured "government," whose primary functions are to provide:

1. Access to His promises and destiny (Hebrews 11:33)
2. A road map for living (Psalm 119:105)
3. Divine physical protection (Luke 10:19)
4. Eternal soul salvation (1 Peter 1:9)

Successful navigation of His kingdom means simply this: "You are in His will." Being in His will can be characterized by three specific things, although there are more requirements. The three main guidelines are that you: (1) Follow the rules of engagement; (2) adhere to the moral code of conduct; and (3) Learn to perfect its prescribed decorum or ways of interacting.

To sum it all up, at best, you begin to think, behave, and interact like the King. Kings and queens have dominion or authority in a kingdom.

> A kingdom consists of a king with citizens. Citizenship is essentially a legal entity with rights and privileges protected by constitutional commitment of a king and his government. (Monroe, Rediscovering the Kingdom, 41.)

How does this kingdom concept explain our position as believers in God's kingdom? Here is one view. Royal monarchs relegate authority based on generational familial rights. We too, as sons of God, possess the same rights in God's kingdom. Therefore, whatever the king grants us rights to perform, we do so with the same authority. After all, we are citizens of His kingdom. The king and his domain describes the governing authority from which citizens draw their right to rule, possess, and take dominion. No other entity in a kingdom can match the authority and power of the king, and no person outside the kingdom shares the same rights as its citizens.

Kingdom of God

Citizens in the kingdom of God are heirs to royal priesthood. Discovering your inherent birthright will position you to embrace the proper perspective concerning your role in the kingdom: royal priesthood. Humility positions us for royal priesthood. No more is kingship measured by the biblical-historical elitism we typically assigned to royalty of that time. You may remember learning about the superficial posture and special rights those in rule assumed during biblical times as their position, sustained solely by birthright, made them the ones everyone tuned in to and should follow. Fluff included. In other words, elaborately dressed, gas-faced prudes some countries' residents choose to relegate authority to (I love England; honestly, I do) is not a depiction of what God's kingdom is like. Kingship isn't marked by an upturned nose, a speculative glance, or posture of superficial grandeur. Peacock strut? Forget about it! It's not an us-versus-them judgmental comparison; neither is it a dinner-table keeping-up-with-the-Joneses discussion of the haves and have-nots.

Have you ever wondered about people who seemingly have a special relationship with God that only they and their cronies can obtain and attain? That special way their prayers (not yours) reached the throne of God. That "special" way they say "Hallelujah!" Priesthood is no longer religious tradition asserting special rights some people have over others to access the ear, mind, and heart of God. All believers have this right; therefore, royal priesthood, in its proper perspective, is our birthright. We have to choose to embrace our spiritual inheritance in the same way and to the same degree that Christ did. If you feel like you have to do something other than surrendering your life to God to have an intimate relationship with Him, remember that God is no respecter of persons.

Learning your true, God-ordained authority takes time. It can seem to take a lifetime through a plethora of pitfalls and recovery times, yielding the desire and fortitude to embrace the power that reveals your spiritual birthright. Nevertheless, becoming a quick study of the King's ways and the authority, we have as daughters of the King will mark you as a purposeful woman of destiny.

Kingdom Operation

There's nothing mystical about understanding the structure of God's kingdom. You might glean comparisons from other forms of government. Take me, for example. As an American citizen, I identity myself as such, not only because it's my birthplace but also because I am American in customs, values, mores, and expression. National pride does not make me American. Instead, this categorization and identification occurs as I model standards set by this nation, standards adhered to within my community networks, and guidelines regarded as standards in my family. It also comes to bear through codes of conduct reinforced in my workplace and place of worship.

Likewise, God's kingdom has "disciples" of Jesus or citizens of the kingdom (Philippians 3:20–21). A disciple is a citizen of the kingdom of God whose primary goal is to model ways of God. Kingdom citizens do this by:

1. Hearing the voice of the Lord and responding (John 10:27)

2. Following the ways of Jesus Christ (Matthew 16:24)
3. Inheriting the Kingdom of God (Matthew 25:34)

What better person to model successful Kingdom living right before His disciples than Jesus Himself? How grateful we are as believers for the recorded writings of several key disciples! Within the gospels, we have seated before us God, the Father, and Jesus, His Son, who is seated at His Father's right hand, with whom we share equal kingdom rights.

> Then shall the King say unto them on his right hand, Come, ye blessed of my Father; inherit the kingdom prepared for you from the foundation of the world. (Matthew 25:34)

Culture created within communities connects people to a particular entity or institution. Likewise, our connection to the kingdom of God and all its promises identifies us as heirs of the kingdom and joint heirs with Jesus Christ. Operating outside the principles governing His kingdom puts you at risk of being outside His will. And yes, there are certainly consequences when we operate outside of His will. As women of the kingdom, we should feel ill-fitted to follow any other standard.

> Cast not away therefore your confidence, which hath great recompense of reward. So that when you have DONE the will of God you may receive what was promised. (Hebrews 10:36)

Identity through Jesus Christ

Discover Jesus. God reveals His will and purpose through Jesus. What was Jesus's role in the plan God predestined for each of us? Discovering God's purpose for humanity starts with His plan for reconciliation, which, through the sacrifice of Jesus, began before earth was created.

> According as he hath chosen us in him before the foundation of the world, that we should be holy and without blame before him in love: Having predestinated

us unto adoption of children by Jesus Christ to himself, according to the good pleasure of his will; To the praise of the glory of his grace, wherein he hath made us accepted in the beloved. (Ephesians 1:5-6)

From "glory to glory" explains the process a spiritually maturing woman undergoes as she discovers her true identity in Christ, one established long before this earth, as we know it today or read about it in science books, was ever created. Who could have known our relationship with Jesus Christ makes us joint heirs to God's promises?

He gave us Jesus, the ultimate example to follow when our journey becomes filled with obstacles.

We put feet to our Christian walk by living what Jesus spoke. When we stumble and make missteps, mercy and forgiveness through Jesus's sacrifice assure perfect forgiveness and forgetting in the eyes our heavenly Father. Perfection is not our goal. Perfect forgiveness means God never goes back on His promise to forgive us for our missteps when we venture outside His will and restores us in right standing with him when we repent.

Father God rates the success of our destiny walk by obedience to His will for our lives. Through Jesus's example, our way is much clearer. Not perfection, only Jesus's way provides the perfect template from which we must construct our personal destiny missions. Therefore, based on our relationships with God and Jesus, we understand better the purpose of Jesus Christ coming as the Messiah.

The primary purposes of Jesus's coming are to give humanity:

1. Power over death and works of evil (Hebrew 3:14)
2. Sanctification through His sufferings (Hebrew 3:11)
3. Freedom from bondage (Hebrew 2:15)
4. Reconciliation for sins (Hebrew 2:17)

Holy Spirit Inspiration

Jesus epitomizes the most superior example of purpose-driven living. The Holy Spirit reveals inspiration or adds meaning and provides how-tos that help guide our walk toward destiny. The Holy Spirit intercedes to God on our behalf, and He becomes our teacher of spiritual things (1 Chronicles

2:13), brings truth through revelation (2 Thessalonians 2:13), and as we come into the knowledge of God's plan for our lives, the Holy Spirit provides comfort to us in our journey (John 14:16).

What spiritual lessons does the Holy Spirit teach us? Some may wonder as breathing, speaking, living people how someone we cannot see can make such an impact upon our lives.

First, God commissions the Holy Spirit to forge the fruit of the Spirit within us. Through the Holy Spirit, God has put a demand on us to produce fruit of salvation (Acts 1:8, 2 Corinthians 3:3), fruit of the Spirit (Galatians 5:22–23), and fruit of good works (Colossians 1:10).

One thing I rest in is this: "All things work together for the good for those [loving God wholly] and are called according to His purpose" (Romans 8:28). After all, God had an established purpose for "being," which is, through Jesus to reconcile everyone's heart back to Himself. In various strategic methods, He employs the Holy Spirit to bring about reconciliation. As we submit our will to God's, the Holy Spirit gently invades our "soulish" space, the seat of our minds, will, and emotions. There, the spirit of holiness (an actual spirit of light; 1 Peter 1:2) makes a seed deposit as we submit to His prompting.

In our submission, the Holy Spirit produces fruit; we cannot do this in our own power. The Holy Spirit's power to renew and regenerate the human heart creates in us new affections, those consistent with the Spirit of God and the His kingdom. Then and only then do we become unified with godly affections also known as the fruit of the spirit. I love how R. A. Torrey explains it in The Presence & Work of the Holy Spirit:

> In the new birth, a new intellectual, emotional and discretionary nature is imparted to us. We receive the mind that sees as God sees, that thinks God's thoughts after Him ... Receive affections in harmony the affections of God ... a will that is in harmony with the will of God, that delights to do the things that please Him ... It is the Holy Spirit who creates this new nature in us, or imparts this new nature to us. It is He, alone, who makes a man a new creature. (p. 99)

The Holy Spirit has many attributes such as comforter and teacher; however, purposes of the Holy Spirit are to:

1. Form the Spirit of Christ within us (Galatians 2:20)
2. Bring forth Christlike graces of character in the believer (Galatians 5:22–23)
3. Bear witness to our sonship (Romans 8:14)
4. Convict the world and set the believer free from the power of sin (Romans 8:2)

GOD'S PURPOSE FOR MANKIND

What is our individual contribution to God's collective plan? As purpose seekers, ladies, we must always stick with what's foundational: God's original plan. As women, we were "originally intended" to efficiently "steward" God's resources (Proverbs 31), taking dominion over key territories (book of Esther) with his good-news message, and mentoring younger women to do the same (Titus 2).

Ladies, this is not a message of religion but of reconciliation, and we all have a role to play in turning people's heart back to God. Preaching and teaching the good news or gospel of Jesus Christ is not limited to those well-versed in theological studies. Interchurch ministry is only one well-respected office of many inside God's kingdom. After all, and in actuality, we are the church. Tools for spreading the good news of the kingdom work as a vast, well-structured machine, which Jesus described through parables in ninety-two scriptural references and sixty-nine exact phrases in the King James Bible.

These descriptions provide many ways that we are expected to hear and to apply the message of the kingdom, and most importantly, they outline how we can employ our unique gifts and talents to bring about His overall purpose collectively. Cookie-cutter formulas and recipes are not necessary; God requires diversity in bringing about His plan through those who are willing to seek and hear His directives. Do not be deceived; most assuredly, fulfilling His divine plan of reconciliation for the kingdom must happen through y-o-u. After all, the kingdom of God is inside of you (Luke 17:21), and His chosen vessel, meaning you, is His most prized treasure.

Preach and Teach the Gospel

Are we all intended to spread the gospel of Christ? Yes, of course! Now that we understand that we are created to spread the good news of the gospel, knowing its ultimate impact will do several things. I know I've struggled personally with this one. Because the bulk of my time and interests revolved around secular activities outside of the church, I did not feel I fit in at all with the context of the local church as we know it today.

In angst, often wondering if I was expected to be the next female missionary, pastor, or small-group leader, I didn't really know what to do or who to turn to. What is a woman without a ministry-related background to think about this? Like many committed to our faith, I was completely baffled. Where exactly did I fit? Was I expected to fit? More than anything else, where did God want me to fit?

Administering Reconciliation

For the woman who still struggles with knowing her place in the kingdom, consider this message Isaiah declared from understanding his purpose in the kingdom:

> The spirit of the Lord has come upon me because He has anointed me to preach the good tidings to the poor; He has sent me to heal the brokenhearted; To proclaim liberty the captives, And the opening of the prison to those who are bound; To proclaim the acceptable year of the LORD, And the day of vengeance of our God; To comfort all who mourn, To console those who mourn in Zion, To give them beauty for ashes; The oil of joy for mourning, The garment of praise for the spirit of heaviness; That they may be called trees of righteousness, The planting of the Lord that He may be glorified. (Isaiah 61: 1–3)

Clearly, all have a place in carrying out healing, restoration, and providing freedom to others, regardless of our occupations. For example, a tax attorney or financial adviser is skilled in providing debt freedom to those who may have fallen on financial tough times. Teachers not only impart knowledge to students but also provide a sense of security and self-esteem to those who fully embrace each lesson. Ask an illiterate person who reads for the first time what new freedom she experiences!

Likewise, governmental public-service providers restore communities as they scrutinize, resolve, and administer pertinent answers for critical issues affecting the populace. Careful decision making in government has great impact on crime, unemployment, and education. While we have seen the down side of faulty judgment in government, this does not negate God's original intent.

> And we know that all things work together for good to those who love God, to those who are the called according to [His] purpose. (Romans 8:28)

Consider your own contribution to His overall plan. Purpose would have it that God's strategic placement of His daughters in key areas of government and education fortify His overall plan for His kingdom. We are made aware of His plan first through personal evaluation, and then the effect of this is experienced through our families, our neighborhoods, our cities, and ultimately, our nation. Integral to our walk in purpose are those spiritual leaders and mentors who, directed by God, through faith, speak into our lives, directing us in kingdom integrity or the way in which we craft our attitudes, and motivation to strengthen God's agenda. These positive effects will produce global impact as we unite in common purpose through varied abilities. Knowledge is indeed empowering.

Build Up the Kingdom

Are we all required to become church workers? No. What if you feel your purpose is not ministry related? If your core calling is not to preach or teach in a church, how then will you contribute to God's overall plan? Start with the practical first. What do you enjoy? What makes you most angry, righteously indignant? Which problems do you solve with ease? The answers to these questions are the beginning of uncovering the purpose of God for your life.

FINDING MY PLACE IN THE KINGDOM OF GOD

What's My Purpose?

The best way to find the will of God for your life is through living. That's it? Yes. That's it, plain and simple. Keep living, breathing, moving, and doing, and God's plan reveals itself in doing very ordinary things. Generally, these ordinary things might be something we do in an extraordinary way. When we do ordinary things with God's enablement or anointing on our lives, what seems ordinary becomes miraculous. The things we take for granted like teaching children, the passion we have for caring for the sick or elderly, our love for art, humanity, and diverse cultures can uncover our hidden purposes for being. Our passion for justice, equity, and righteousness also is an indicator of where God is directing us. Empathizing with emotional hurt in others extends past making yourself available to be a listening ear. All our passions, gifts, and talents pave the road we travel called destiny and purpose.

It's not science, really. But you can get your walk-in purpose down to a science. Unlike science, nothing is ever hidden from us; however, to discover the plan of God, we must pursue, search out, explore, and develop what is already given to us: a life full of possibilities. Coupled with our own personal desires, talents, and skills, we all can uncover God's purpose for our lives.

I know. Few people make this clear. Discovering our reason for being isn't limited to a few select, super-spiritual, well-mentored persons. It is essential, though, to seek God for wisdom and others for guidance. We do need this part. It's one of the most practical rules on the road to purpose.

Collective Versus Individual Purposes

God-ordained collective and individual purposes do not change. We become aware of dual purposes, which complement God's overall design of His kingdom, only by revelation gained through fellowship with Him and studying His Word. Other factors such as unique gifting and abilities we possess, along with proper mentorship, will help align us on our destiny path.

Purpose and Mission: What's the Difference?

Unlike our collective and individual purposes, our missions change. Personal missions change as we move from one assignment to the next. Our company culture takes on the form of God's kingdom-of-heaven agenda.

As a company will revamp its mission statement to allow for growth and expanded services, we should likewise update our personal mission to gain a fuller picture of the ever-evolving plan for our lives. Core features of company mission remain the same; however, the methods, procedures, and products used to support cultural demands must change with the needs of the population the company serves. Mission statements, usually broadly defined, reflect agreement on a few core principles.

For example, companies use creative ways to garner customer satisfaction, production efficiency, and value pricing. Company branding marks the how, what, when, where, and which that informs decision makers about the process of developing mission statements. How are we "branded" as godly women destined to complete, not compete, with God's kingdom agenda? We are marked as His righteousness and praise of His glory! What is the kingdom culture demanding and putting pressure on us to produce? Works and fruit of the spirit align God's kingdom agenda. To discover what it really takes to become one of God's most prized "public relations representatives" on walking in purpose, read ahead to the discussion on kingdom integrity (chapters 9 and 10). In the meantime, let's reflect on what was discussed in this chapter.

POT OF PREPARATION STEW REFLECTION

Many ingredients go into purpose's pot of preparation stew. Let's begin with the first one. As chapter 1 not so subtly alludes to, ladies, we must continually "bring forth fruit" (John 15:16). But wait! Before you start envisioning fruit orchards, we're not talking apples and oranges, "But the fruit of the Spirit is love, joy, peace, longsuffering, gentleness, goodness, faith" (Galatians 5:22). Are you wondering "What exactly does this have to do with my walk in purpose?" Okay, let's start with the long answer. It's foundational to embracing our inherent birthright as "sons" of God and provides proof that God made carrying out His will for our lives doable (reliable), and if we follow the plan and use the proper tools, we get the right (valid) results.

> Ye have not chosen me, but I have chosen you, and ordained you, that ye should go and bring forth fruit, and [that] your fruit should remain: that whatsoever ye shall ask of the Father in my name, he may give it you. (John 15:16)

The short answer is you are chosen! However, there are special conditions God's chosen ones must meet to receive His promise: "Whatsoever ye shall ask of the Father in my name, he will give it." Satisfying these conditions means something is required from us, which is, we must "bear" and have lingering ("remaining") fruit.

It's Your Turn

Think about it. Considering the role of the Holy Spirit as the fruit of the spirit cultivator, examine your prayer life. Examine the following questions. After reading chapter 1:

1. What does it mean to you to pursue purpose with a kingdom-centric perspective?
2. How important is regular, God-directed intercession in order for you to get the right perspective on life?
3. Regarding your walk in purpose, how does godly confidence give you the power to overcome personal weaknesses?

Begin with these questions, and then pray for God to reveal to you His plan for your life.

PRAYER FOR UNLOCKING GOD'S PROMISES

Father, please forgive me for not seeing more sides of You. No longer will I overlook the fullness of who You are, and through Your Son, Jesus Christ, I claim my inherent birthright. As I pursue Your presence, restore me in right standing with You. Align my path in righteousness as I submit to honoring You with my obedience. Unlock the promise already inside of me; therefore, restore the dreams You've place inside of me. Renew my mind to reflect heaven's agenda for me and my higher purpose. Position me in humility so that I may posture myself in power, glory, authority, and high honor as a son of God (female and male). Thank You, Father, for performing what You have already spoken about me before the beginning of time. Amen.

CHAPTER 2

PATIENCE

CROCK-POT®

Purposeful Women
Submit to Lengthy Times of Preparation

God's timing mimics, in some ways, creating a meal in a slow cooker. In the recipe for "purpose's preparation stew," the beef, carrots, and potatoes—the ingredients in a homemade beef stew recipe—represent experiences, gifts, and talents. Personality, like a robust heap of seasoning, adds that special spark to life's journey. Bless the cook whose hands prepare delicious beef stew. Thank goodness, throwing in a handful of wonderfully mixed seasonings makes a succulent, tummy-filling, and delectable delight.

FRUIT OF THE SPIRIT CHECK: PATIENCE

Be assured and understand that the trial and proving of your faith bring out endurance and steadfastness and patience. But let endurance and steadfastness and patience have full play and do a thorough work, so that you may be [people] perfectly and fully developed [with no defects], lacking in nothing. (James 1:2–4 AMP)

There's one thing. Preparing a hearty beef stew takes time and takes an even longer time, so it seems, if you've skipped lunch. It seems to take much too long if you've had an earlier breakfast. What's more tempting than the scent of aromatic beef stew slowly cooking, simmering? Then experiencing gradually intensifying gnawing hunger pangs that are sure to follow.

Then, you see it. Like Saturday morning cartoons, a pot full of beef stew's aroma coming alive is like this smoky arm and hand figure beckoning—come hither. In reality, this is only an illusion, competing for space in your senses. Clearly, there is no way to reduce the wait time for something scrumptious and satisfying and achieve the same quality results.

Slow-cooked meals require patience; so does pursuing purpose. Hard-won wisdom always trumps illusion, doesn't it? This chapter will outline practical principles governing God's timing.

God's Timing: The Slow Cooker

Slow cookers, referred to as Crock-Pots® are slow, and so is pursuing purpose, according to God's timing. Be encouraged! As a simmering stew creates a much richer flavor, patiently submitting to God's preparation produces what it takes to walk out purpose in a more meaningful way. Operating in excellence brings honor to the part of destiny's plan God created you to fulfill.

The Thing About Waiting Is …

The process of waiting often masquerades as the proverbial wet blanket thrown on the fire of one's pursuit. This is understandable; no one enjoys waiting—period. It simply takes too long to get where we are going, and then there's added time in understanding what we are supposed to do when we get there. Besides, while waiting, we rarely know precisely what we are waiting for anyway. Acknowledging this, however, makes this reality no less disheartening, but we revel in knowing that the really big and exciting thing we are waiting for is chock full of purpose. We want the big *it*, and we want it right now. Like yesterday.

> Between the wish and the thing, life lays waiting.
> —Unknown

Is there any real significance in waiting for our God-given purposes? If there is, then what is it? Whenever we speak of God's timing to define a specific period set apart from others, we use terms such as the "right season," "destiny," and "for such a time as this." Also included in God's timing is an intense "season of preparation." This season makes it easy to overlook the critical importance of preparation time needed to be trained, because we become frustrated and disillusioned by the process that He takes us through to qualify us for the "big *it*."

Which experiences are preparing you for your purpose? Will you wait patiently to find purpose in them? There simply are no shortcuts, none at all.

SEASONS OF PREPARATION

Waiting Reveals Purpose

Christian cinema recently captured the "timing of God" motif. *One Night with the King* chronicles Queen Esther's on-time intercession on behalf of the Jewish people, a masterfully orchestrated plan to save the Jewish people of Persia. On the other hand, the Bible narrative of the five virgins shows readers what it takes to properly prepare for a marriage feast. Two such examples paint very different pictures of God's (much-needed) interruption upon the timing of critical events on our road to purpose and destiny.

Chronicled in the story of Esther is a fine example of God's sovereign hand upon timing. Upon first reading the account in the book of Esther, it appears that Esther's purpose was to marry King Xerxes, the outrageously handsome, wealthy man whose former wife, Vashti, brought him public dishonor when she refused to come to his party, a bold act of disobedience at this time.

However, this was not an intentional plan at all; rather, it can be described as a vivid representation of how the coming together of the right persons, right circumstances, and right timing brings about God's will. Esther was assigned a task, and her silent partner, the Spirit of God— although God's name is not mentioned in the book of Esther— showed His sovereign work at hand. Esther not only gained access into King Xerxes's palace but also into his heart. Convinced of Esther's pure intentions, Xerxes halted Haman's plan to annihilate the Jewish people, which began long before Esther's coming to "save much people alive" (Genesis 50:20) "for such a time as this" (Esther 4:14). God's timing always precludes or overrules circumstances.

Purposed Assignments

Whether it's Esther, the five virgins, or a woman spearheading a national committee, God strategically prepares us for greatness through a series of well-designed assignments. In the introduction, we learned that God has a collective and an individual plan for our lives. Within these plans are many carefully planned assignments.

Here's another thing. Assignments are time-sensitive. Be careful not to find yourself stuck in your assignment! I can speak personally to the disappointment and anguish experienced when doors of opportunity closed on God-given assignments. When I thought relationships, jobs, and volunteer opportunities would last forever, or at least until I felt the need to do something else, something better that suited my fancy, more often than not, they were altered or changed altogether before I anticipated they would.

My life belongs to God, and yours does too. Move swiftly! God's next level of promotion awaits you.

Responding quickly to change will lessen confusion. That's what happens when you begin parsing facts, analyzing each minute detail of your experiences, and engaging in mental charades to make those seemingly illogical pieces of life fit together. They will not fit. Life simply does not make sense all the time, and when it does not, you begin questioning when, how, why, and what in the world happened.

I have been there too many times to count. You have been there, also. We are women, and Details 'R' Us! Women have a propensity toward tidbit-recall. God created this trait within us to operate as exquisite life managers; however, naturally, as the saying goes, too much of a good thing can and will be our downfall, if we let it. Don't let it. Follow God's plan; leave the details to Him.

> We must be willing to get rid of the life we've planned, so as to have the life that is waiting for us. —Joseph Campbell (1904–1987)

So what does this interruption in our groove teach us? Well, first, there is obviously some other force at work behind the scenes. Plus, as we try our hardest to set sail in a bright white boat, on perfectly buoyant waters, on a perfectly brisk Sunday at the lake, God determines our destination (if we allow), and the rate in which our boat travels (if we grant Him captain's rights). What may seem like sabotage or a well-aimed monkey wrench in our perfect plan is simply God redirecting our course. Many times we are not off course, just not on our course.

Ladies, let's go with the flow. Do not let your quest for perfection become an enemy to your destiny's journey. Besides, we all know we've messed up things all on our own. It's only after we've exhausted all our efforts and flown a white flag of surrender that God's hands replace ours as helmsman to steer us safely along the nautical miles of our life's journey.

Preparing for a Greater Purpose

In the Parable of the Ten Virgins, Jesus revealed a principle of the kingdom of heaven in Matthew 25:1–13) as ten virgin brides awaited the marriage feast. In this parable, we notice four keys illuminating this point. Preparing for God's purpose requires that you know God's:

1. Wise preparation for the assigned task
2. Signal for timing on assignments
3. Heart regarding proper preparation, and
4. Method of identifying and overcoming potential distractions

> Then shall the kingdom of heaven be likened unto ten virgins, which took their lamps, and went forth to meet the bridegroom. (Matthew 25:1)

IDENTIFYING THE TIMING OF YOUR ASSIGNMENT

Five of the ten virgin brides knew what time it was! The other "foolish" five seemingly missed a grand opportunity to join the others at the marriage feast (Matthew 25:2). What made them so foolish? Was it the lack of proper planning and faulty preparation, perhaps? Those left-out five virgins neglected the assignment to fill their candle lamps:

Five of them were foolish, and five were wise. But while they were gone to buy oil, the bridegroom came. Then those who were ready went in with him to the marriage feast, and the door was locked. Later, when the other five bridesmaids returned, they stood outside, calling, "Lord! Lord! Open the door for us!" (Matthew 25:2, 10–11).

Prepare Wisely

How many times have you overlooked God's prompting to _____ ? (You fill in the blank.) It's true that five of the ten virgins slothfully prepared for the bridegroom, while "the other five were wise enough to take along extra oil" (Matthew 25:2). All ten virgins knew the bridegroom's arrival was nearing, and although He delayed the feast, soon after, all ten virgins were alerted to his arrival with a "[rousing] shout." They all heard the call (Matthew 25:6).

Learn God's Heart on Matters

To know God's heart is to know God's ways. This parable describes the consequences for those most and least prepared for Christ's coming. Those who were out buying oil rather than burning oil at the right time missed the opportunity. Here's the practical significance of this parable. Despite obvious hindrances, the most critical mistake the foolish virgins made was that they did not know the bridegroom's desires, did not know his heart.

Let me explain. Relating to our closest friends and family members is certainly not without challenges. Let's face it, maintaining healthy relationships takes real work and sometimes extreme personal sacrifice. However, the point here is this: few of us sustain relationships without knowing the personal desires of the people with whom we connect. Knowing another's heart—what pleases him; what makes her feel loved, valued, and appreciated is made known through open communication, not mind reading. It is then less complex to think ahead about what might please them.

Watch for the Signs

For Esther, sounds of Jewish pilgrims assembling themselves to take the yearly caravan to Jerusalem signaled the beginning of her culture-altering efforts to stay the hand of a vicious attack upon the Israelites. The "signal" occurred after King Cyrus's decree, and Israelite exiles were allowed to return to their native Jerusalem (Ezra 1). Many chose to remain in Babylon.

Sounds of caravans also marked the time for Jewish families to come together and memorialized events after King Cyrus's conquest of Babylon (539 BC), the new homeland of many exiled Israelites. Unaware of the significance, at the time, Esther's placement into King Xerxes's royal harem, and then her rise to queen as a replacement for ousted Queen Vashti also indicated that God was up to something amazing. He'd systematically orchestrated its occurrence! These events taking place to bring about His plan through a young orphan girl named Esther were no coincidence.

Just as the ten virgins followed signs of the soon-coming bridegroom, women would be wise to become aware of the practical ways God's timing reveals itself. Unfortunately, only five virgins responded by readying themselves to enter the feast. Five virgin bridesmaids had enough oil to supply their lamps and gained entrance to the feast; the other five did not and distracted themselves by trekking to the local shop to purchase more oil. They missed their divine appointment.

Minimize Distractions

Distractions are potential blockers to progressing in God's timing. Learning which attitudes and behaviors hinder us is critical to pursuing purpose. In the case of the virgin bridesmaids, knowing what protocol to follow would have made preparing for the marriage feast much easier, right? Bring ample oil to light the lamp and await the call seems simple enough, but some did not follow the instructions and missed the feast.

Nothing is worse than preparing for a spectacular event to which you have been invited and not being able to attend because of your own slothfulness.

What is the reason you missed it? Did you get the wrong time? Had you received the invitation but on the day of the event got caught up doing last-minute hullabaloo, everyday life "noise" that has nothing to do with your path to purpose? I love the way Eli said it in the motion picture The Book of Eli, starring Denzel Washington: "This has nothing to do with me. Stay on the path." Focus on the plan, opportunity, and assignment. Focus on your purpose, and pray earnestly against distractions. Stay on your course.

CROCK-POT® REFLECTION

As chapter 2 illustrates, as kingdom purpose seekers, women must not only commit proper time to honing their skills and talents and availing themselves of opportunities and experiences that will place them in the right position, but they must also recognize the signs that announce the coming of the opportunity. Once you recognize the opportunity, you must fight with all your might to maintain patient resolve and the endurance to see the assignment through, no matter how long it takes.

It's Your Turn

There is a limit to everyone's endurance, but there's also something God deems magnificent about waiting.

> Who would have guessed it possible that waiting is sustainable? A place with its own harvest. —Kay Ryan, poet

The endurance it takes to process through each carefully crafted, God-directed stage of life does something wonderful for the human spirit. The product of such deliberate processing makes us, His chosen ones, "perfect and fully developed" (James 1:2–4) to execute the tasks that He has set before us. In theory, we know it's best to do it His way, but what this does to the human will can be, shall we say, excruciating!

The popular Arabian idiom, "the straw that broke the camel's back," illustrates what can happen when we, as purposeful women, seemingly carry the burden of our destiny on our backs. O, Lord! That too! When we are already so filled with purpose, a single proverbial straw can compete with our natural ability to stay the full course and endure. Ponder these questions:

1. Can you recall a time when you had to turn down what appeared to be a perfect opportunity for one that was a God opportunity? What deciding factors did you consider to make the distinction? Was the outcome a fulfilling one that brought greater clarity to God's purpose for your life?
2. How might balancing priorities (God's versus ours) help us lighten the load as we patiently allow God to prepare us for the next task? Is it very easy to make this determination? Why or why not?

Remember, the "weight of responsibility" for carrying out a task is God's, and all He needs from you is patience to stay in the "camel caravan" (or race) and endure to the end.

PRAYER FOR ENDURANCE

"Dear Lord, thank you for giving me the strength and the conviction to complete the tasks You entrusted to me. Thank You for guiding me straight and truly through the many obstacles in my path and for keeping me resolute when all around seemed lost. Thank You for Your protection and Your many signs along the way. I fought the good fight; I finished the race; I kept the faith." (The Book of Eli, Gary Whitta, 2010)

CHAPTER 3

PRESSURE

POT TIMER

Purposeful Women
Know God's Principles Governing Timing

"What do you have for me today?" Puzzled by the request of the assertive, pink-clad, five-year-old girl, Janessa scurried to come up with a suitable response.

"Ohm, well, let me see." Janessa pondered briefly and then decided she had not a clue what the young girl needed, wanted, or required. "What would you like?" Janessa said, now leaning forward, eye to eye with her.

Again, the young girl persisted, hand extended forward. "I know you have something for me today! Where is it?" Standing with her hand on her hip and outstretched slender arms, resembling spaghetti, she wouldn't let down. Putting pressure on her to produce something, anything challenged Janessa to perform and do it quickly!

By this time, Janessa knew she had better find something, anything, so she reached inside her purse and discovered a round, cellophane-wrapped peppermint ball. "Here you go!"

Gleaming, the young girl quickly grabbed the mint ball as if it were some valued treasure.

"See. I knew you had something for me!"

FRUIT OF THE SPIRIT CHECK: PEACE

> And the peace of God, which passeth all understanding, shall keep your hearts and minds through Christ Jesus. (Philippians 4:7)

After hearing this anecdote from my friend Janessa, I thought about the value of childlike innocence. Think for a moment. If we all had the same persistence as the young girl, all that we desired would be pursued and obtained gracefully, especially those things in line with our purpose and passion where persistence counts. God does indeed have something very special for you. Pursue it with boldness as you wait for that "something just for me" to show up for you.

PRINCIPLES GOVERNING GOD'S TIMING

What is God's timing, and for what are we waiting? No matter what, we must submit to the process. I know this will take some getting used to, but it's well worth it once we know that waiting on God's purpose is not passive submission. Instead, waiting on God to reveal His plan and His way gives credence to the notion that His process is so much better than ours. He's always right; therefore, knowing which principles govern His process empowers us with the tools we need to master our walk in purpose. These tools reveal themselves as we identify which of the four seasons of purpose we are embarking upon:

1. Call
2. Preparation
3. Commission
4. Send

These seasons are not narrowly defined at all, but generally, purpose seekers identify themselves in one of these four categories at some point in their lifetimes. More commonly, however, the preparation stage is continuous and precedes periods in which we must qualify for specific assignments or tasks. Completing an assignment qualifies us for the next. Remember, God's criteria are not a pass-or-fail scoring but obedience. In obedience, we submit to "the process," taking into consideration the following stages.

The Call

Answering "the call" means you have asked yourself the question "What problems am I passionate about solving?" In the introduction, we discussed that our natural gifts and talents align the thing God has called us to complete, our purpose for living in God's will. After we identify these—which sometimes change as we become aware of His plan for our lives—we are chosen to prepare for the next stages of our walk in purpose. Obedience to His plan positions us as "chosen" persons mentioned in Matthew 22:14. Furthermore, God's chosen fruit meets the highest of standards and survives the most vigorous processing (Matthew 22:11–14).

Preparation

Next, "precious preparation" is the time that we yield to God's unique processing, making us suitable and fit for His use. Included in this period is something I call "Tender Time." I define Tender Time as "a time reserved to covet waiting, to allow the Holy Spirit to sharpen your character and integrity and hone your gifting." This period is not without testing. Even the disciples were tested before becoming dynamic leaders. This time marks the period right before commission, when we begin to imitate the ways of Jesus and take hold of the mind of Christ.

Commission

"Cultivating greatness" means our walk in purpose mimics the farmer awaiting his fall harvest. Seed time (or seed and time), and then harvest describes this process. This stage of preparation requires sowing seed in the right soil (fertile ground) and tending to what we have sown in order to produce sprouts at the right time. Fruit is harvested in the right or ripe season (Matthew 13–18). God sets the timetable when it is time to harvest the crop. Queen Esther attended her coronation ceremony (Esther 2:17–19) (commission ceremony) prior to taking her seat of authority as God's honorable vessel.

Send

Becoming a vessel of honor requires purity and consecration. After harvesting the fruit, what vessel is suitable to contain it? This vessel is one that is cleansed and fit for the Master's use (2 Timothy 2:21). Chapter 7 outlines what a vessel of honor is and how to identify what is required to become a woman of integrity. What makes us vessels of honor as we walk in purity, sanctification, and holiness?

REIGNING IN GOD'S TIMING

How do you know you are ripe for the picking? There are certain tell-tale signs for discerning when you are in God's timing for a specific assignment. Some signs present themselves in a subtle way; others shout for recognition. "It's time for the harvest! All your preparation paid off! You are exactly who God planned you to be!" Your life will radiate the kind of glory only God can bestow upon His chosen women.

"That is enough. No more pressure, please!" While in God's timing of preparation, opportunities for accountability increase because God now trusts you. He gives you more responsibility, and with more responsibility comes added pressure. With added pressure comes the opportunity for offenses, distractions, and missteps. Watch out for the pitfalls! Just remember that an opportunity is something one either embraces or doesn't. Embrace what's acceptable to God; reject all else.

Opportunities Increase

1. Accountability in workplaces, volunteering, ministry, and family contexts increase.
2. Personal offenses increase as more responsibility forges the need for personal growth.

3. Distractions enter when we let our guard down, when we become tired, or lack proper balance to handle added responsibilities.

4. Potential for missteps increase as we are presented with too many "good" options.

"Um, I will pass. I don't want to do this anymore." When God's perfect timing is upon our lives, we are often wooed by the Holy Spirit to live a consecrated lifestyle, not through religious sacrifice but through sheer obedience to God's purpose. Our desires change.

Your Desires Change Toward:

1. Activities you've enjoyed in the past
2. People who are experiencing the same rapturous delight
3. Mind-sets reflecting God's kingdom agenda

Bless God for all the great things He has done! In God's timing, we begin to see the hand of God at work in our lives, and for this, we develop unusual gratitude. Gratitude and "humility precedes honor" (Proverbs 15:33).

Unusual Gratitude for:

1. God's favor upon your life
2. Involvement in ministry/leadership activities
3. God's intervention upon the critical events in your life

"Mirror, mirror on the wall, who is that person looking back at me?" We begin to reflect the kind of person God needs to carry out His perfect will in His timing. It is not about personal preferences and style, or even background, although God uses our unique traits to bring about His will. In the mirror, we see a person who reflects God and His purposes!

Reflecting God's:

1. Character
2. Heart (not just a heart for God, but the heart of God)
3. Passions and desires to meet the needs of the people and entities you serve

Honestly, there are no templates, prescribed plans, explicit instructions, or time-tested escape routes (for she who has become overwhelmed in the journey) for processing through each invisible yet undoubtedly real stage of purpose. However, an encouraged heart and peaceful spirit is one that knows that while walking in purpose is not for the faint of heart, what's most important is not perfection but a fixed mind to respond properly.

Let's take a look at Pot Timer Reflections to see how you fare.

POT TIMER REFLECTIONS

I absolutely love chapter 3! It gets down to the nuts and bolts of what this walk in purpose really entails. Chapter 3 outlines the nitty-gritty of what those who are honest about this destiny thing really experience, an inside look at what pressure we must undergo—and relays a very critical message: purposeful women promptly respond to God's principles regarding timing. How many of us respond gracefully, having to wait patiently and process through who knows how many setbacks and disappointments? Who can forget those distracting moments? For these reasons, we all desperately need the fruit of the Spirit, peace.

It's Your Turn

All right, ladies, let's recap. Distractions are bad news, but few of us can avoid them. There is no need to be thrown completely off track each time a distraction comes, not even a little shaken, if we plan well. Be proactive and plan for distractions. What do I mean? Know up front that everything we do as women of purpose is going to be met with opposition, no matter how special the task before us is. Begin by listing some behaviors and attitudes that might attempt to block your kingdom purpose. I've added a few items to think about. In your quiet time in prayer, ask the Holy Spirit to search your heart to reveal more.

1. Do I lack preparation or motivation for carrying out tasks or assignments?
2. Have I moved out of position or yielded to distractions?
3. Have I failed to change course when needed?

4. What about balancing dual purposes? Am I handling more than one assignment at a time well?
5. Do I know God's will, or am I doing my will?
6. Do I practice forgiveness or become bitter toward correction and setbacks?
7. Do I take it personally when God closes doors that seem to be doors of great opportunity?
8. Do I walk in humility or elevate gifts, talents, and purpose above God's sovereignty?

PRAYER FOR PEACE

Father, You are the Good Shepherd who will never lead me astray. While I may not know where every path I travel will lead me, when I reach the final destination, I know the path You set before me was in Your original plan. Guide my steps; light my way. Help me avoid unnecessary detours and distractions. Give me peace on my journey. Bless me to do good all the days of my life.

CHAPTER 4

PURSUE

POTLUCK

Purposeful Women
Learn to Capitalize on Life's Hodgepodge Experiences

Grandma's quilts are very dear to me. I always look forward to hometown visits to my paternal grandmother's house to envelop myself at bedtime in one of her handmade creations; I love the intricate details. She usually keeps quilts tucked away in a small closet, one stacked atop another. Cube and triangle-shaped gingham, paisley prints, and denim are all carefully sewn together as if the fabrics originally belonged together.

I am amazed at how she mended together several different pieces of fabric from unrelated sources—some dated, some new—to create a beautiful portrait of both color and texture. I would ask Grandma where she had found such interesting fabrics and to what she owed her creative inspiration. Each time, she rendered a different story. Presenting it as new, her story of the quilts did actually seem brand new, just as new as the last time she had told it.

FRUIT OF THE SPIRIT CHECK: GENTLENESS (KINDNESS)

> We should live "in purity, understanding, patience
> and kindness; in the Holy Spirit and in sincere love; in
> truthful speech and in the power of God; with weapons
> of righteousness in the right hand and in the left" (2
> Corinthians 6:6–7).

Not only am I fond of Grandma's quilts, but I also love her tantalizing meals that leave most begging for more—especially those invited to her annual holiday dinners. Even when her guests insisted on bringing a covered dish, she politely refused them, as if to say, "Potluck reserves itself a place at the church social." No hodgepodge at Grandma's table! A kind gesture indeed, offered by her guests, but Grandma values the lasting impact of harmonious flavor. With too many chefs in the kitchen, there is certain discord—again, no hodgepodge at Grandma's table. Together with her gift for quilt making, she has mastered ways to cater to the senses, knowing that only a few can measure up to her skill.

Our experiences are like quilts constructed, and like potluck, one by one we attempt to make sense of our hodgepodge experiences. However, the reality of these experiences might never blend together with quite the same harmony of flavors as Grandma's meals. Nevertheless, just like her tantalizing meals, achieving life's harmony requires deliberate intention. When discovering what great purposes lie behind our ordinary experiences and how they can form the bridge to our extraordinary purpose, we can add meaning to otherwise-confusing realities.

MAKING THE BEST OF HODGEPODGE EXPERIENCES

Change the way you think about your experiences. It might be helpful to extend this principle a step further. Become eager to profit from all of life's hodgepodge experiences. Learning to appreciate good experiences is one thing, but to profit from the good and bad experiences positions us as excellent defensive players in the game of life. In this game, only strategic players called overcomers witness God's promises (Revelation 17:14).

Increasing Your Expectation

Expectation is the bridge linking our hearts' desire to our God-ordained purposes. I believe it is human nature to desire the very best out of life. It is divine to expect the best of life, despite contrary circumstances. In pursuit of the extraordinary, the move from desire to expectation is something most people fail to put into practice. This is by far not a Pollyanna notion, one asserting a view through rose-colored glasses, yearlong peach blossoms in Georgia, a skip through the park while no one is looking. For most, life experiences simply don't transpire quite as easily as this. However, we all do live for wonderful experiences.

Managing Your Perception

Experiences often shape how we view ourselves; if we are not careful, negative experiences can stick to us like mud! This is not what God intends to happen. So-called negative experiences should ultimately translate into learning experiences.

Remember your latest foul-up? How well did you recover, and how long did it take you get back into the swing of things? Was that occurrence really as bad as you thought at the time? Whatever strategy it took you to get back on track, (whether your recovery plan was intentional or not), surely, major perception management was involved. After all, somewhere between expectation and purpose, you will gather tools that will help you to form an accurate perception of what will actually propel your pursuit.

How we see things ultimately forms the pictures we use to summarize our experiences. By these experiences, we gather information. Information gathering during our experiences—good or bad—is an integral part of forming our purpose. We all yearn for purpose. It is simply that the perception of our circumstances seeks to silence our hearts' cry. How many of us remember times when we were deeply bothered by _____ ? (You fill in the blank.)

Profiting from Uncertainty

Some good experiences, some not-so-good ones—we all have them. Somehow, we remember mostly our trials. Although we all fight to maintain belief in the common good, let us be frank; we may not have been as gracefully triumphant in yesterday's circumstances as we are today. Honestly, who is? Yet, even after embracing the benefits of life's lessons we have learned while overcoming our trying times, we still strive to maintain balance amid trials. In personal loss, disappointment, heartache, missed opportunities—occurrences brought on by everyday life—we make the best of most situations, even if at first the thought of doing so is far from us!

CHANGE COURSE IN PURSUIT OF GREATER PURPOSE

I recently attended a home fellowship sponsored by members of a local church. There was nothing particularly religious about the gathering at all, simply ordinary people having ordinary experiences. Each person in attendance sought inspiration. Following a brief lesson, the meeting facilitator opened up a time for final discussion and prayer. Encircled in the tiny space were individuals eager to surrender their hearts' cry to resolution. Prayer requests rang out, one after another.

Everyone nodded in agreement to each petition to God for divine intervention. The requests varied. Some requested more intimacy with God, to know Him better; others prayed for continued blessings over the lives of family members. There were well-known "get me out of trouble, Lord" prayers requested. Outnumbering all requests were the "Lord, rescue me from financial hardship" prayers.

Right before the session ended, a young woman solicited prayer of a different kind. Speaking of her desire to passionately pursue God's will for her life, she had asked for divine wisdom, the leading of God to direct her path. Everyone in attendance listened intently as if singled out individually; familiar was this request to most who have "grandmothered" the Christian walk. Many had already experienced the struggle to maintain balance between God's will and their perceived purpose.

Seemingly, the young woman had given this issue a great deal of forethought. She had acknowledged that it was time to chart a new course. She proclaimed to the group, "I want to do everything with God leading me."

Amen.

Haven't we all made this confession? "I vow to do it God's way. This time, my way isn't quite working."

Despite the resolve to "do it right" this time, the young woman professed disobedience in pursuing her God-destined career. The young woman, Nicole, had convinced herself to change her current profession to pursue one in line with what she thought was God's intended plan. How many of us have plunged straight ahead to do what we thought should be our lifelong purpose? Filled with uncertainty, she desperately needed the assurance of wise counsel. The counsel varied:

- "It time for us in the body of Christ to leave the safety of our nests, our comfort zones," proclaimed a mature woman.
- "If change is in our heart, that indicates that God is challenging us to move to the next level."

The path to the extraordinary is not always clear cut, as one would expect. Nicole had listened fixedly to the words of wisdom, as if being given the verbal passcode to enter a gold-filled vault. No holds barred; she had acknowledged receiving those gems of wisdom! I too listened as Nicole responded to the advice. I could not overlook, however, her repeated reference to having messed up, missed the mark, and being a rebel in the days before she knew Christ. The behavior, she claimed, greatly accounted for her current dilemma. What a punishment for not following God's plan.

An obvious discovery to me, this young woman had a strong, self-condemning awareness! While it is true that we might make entirely different decisions before committing ourselves to a purpose-guided life, even the mishaps are a part of the plan. After all, our bad decisions that seem to be mishaps often propel us into our missions!

Balancing dual purposes, God's will and our will, must be frustrating! God never intended it to be that way. He desires that we become entirely consumed in working out His will for our lives, laying aside all else. Is this easier said than done? Absolutely! All that His plan entails should completely overtake us, so that working to achieve His purpose for our lives tips the scale. Our plan will never register as weight on the balance at all when compared in magnitude to the awesome plan God has for us. I reemphasize my earlier statement: The path to the extraordinary is not always clear cut, as one would expect. Be willing to change courses.

POTLUCK REFLECTIONS

At what point in chapter 4 were you looking for practical instructions for making lemonade out of life's lemons? With talk of food, fun, and fellowship, why not include lemonade to round things off? Life's lemony-sour, and certainly those unpredictable myriad experiences leave much for discussion, filling many books—even noteworthy bestsellers lining the shelves of most bookstores, but not here. Please look further. Further, much further down the book aisle, select another book, two rows over in the self-help section.

I am not at all against inspiration-driven books, as I too believe in the built-in power of positive confession and the efficacy of time-tested how-tos. However, I am impressed mostly by sustainable results that come by way of practical application. There is, without a doubt, nothing more practical than community potluck dinners. It takes the fruit of gentleness to pull purpose out of life's potluck experiences and requires some kind of divine perspective and "power of God; with weapons of righteousness in the right hand and in the left" (2 Corinthians 6:6–7; Ephesians 3:16). That's power!

It's Your Turn

Profiting from Lessons Learned During the Journey

Reflect upon what things you might have learned and have experienced. What was unique or extraordinary about the people you have encountered and the places you have seen? How many lives could you have possibly affected? How many situations could you have affected without even noticing?

PRAYER FOR KINGDOM PURPOSE

Heavenly Father, I thank You that while I am transitioning to the next place of opportunity, promotion, and even enterprise, Your angels are warring for me in the heavens. I thank You that while I assemble all spiritual weapons of warfare, I am also identifying the cracks in my own foundation, places of potential distraction, perfecting my own character in the process. Heavenly Father, I thank You for teaching me to walk in kindness, and valuing each of my life transitions as necessary parts of my walk in kingdom purpose.

CHAPTER 5

POTTER'S WHEEL

POSITION

Purposeful Women
Celebrate Your Unique Contributions to God's Kingdom Agenda

Okay, I admit it: I have always been a bit sappy, even as a little girl, so please bear with me. Realizing that not everyone can appreciate the art of capitalizing upon each minute detail, fluff included, I understand completely. However, for those who revel in finding purpose in even the smallest details (albeit making mountains of molehills), yell out, "I am a purpose seeker!" Did you say it? Feel invigorated? Me too. One more time—"I am a purpose seeker!" Now, it's your turn. Let that proclamation resonate within you. You will need it. Purpose seeking is not for the faint or faithless of heart.

FRUIT OF THE SPIRIT CHECK: JOY

The joy of the Lord is your strength. (Nehemiah 8:10) Let us fix our eyes on Jesus, the author and perfecter of our faith, who for the joy set before him endured the cross, scorning its shame, and sat down at the right hand of the throne of God. (Hebrews 12:2)

Purpose seekers glean from what is seemingly insignificant, ordinary, or even painful or disappointing. Gleaning may come deliberately, as we search for significance, or by happenstance, as we find ourselves in the middle of the unexpected. To glean means to "assemble, bring together, collect, or gather." (Merriam-Webster Dictionary, 2010) In sum, the purpose seeker's mentality is to make the best of every opportunity by gathering what is needed to bring together purposeful meaning from each encounter, despite the outcome.

Once defined, it becomes clearer why purpose seeking becomes an essential part of launching an extraordinary destiny. Are you ready for the ride of your life? Do you promise to buckle up? It's a bumpy road ahead; destination clear? Not really. But clearly, you have a purpose for traveling this path. Godspeed anyway!

DISCOVERING PURPOSE

Feeling especially purposeful one weekend, I began a trek to a foreign land in search of purpose. I am very dramatic; forgive me. Put briefly, I mean I attended a church summer conference scheduled in Virginia. I found out about it from the organization's website and had never been there but was open to something new. The conference speaker lineup was familiar to me, and the theme was too. It seemed like a win-win situation, right?

There was only one small, unknown detail to factor into the whole equation. Laid off from a job with a nonprofit organization just days prior, I grappled with a decision: stay and continue to search for new employment or go while appearing irresponsible for vacationing in place of confirmed employment. Decisions, decisions, decisions! For those who think I went back and forth, pondered long and hard over the decision to travel, guess again. I chose the latter, a decision I was later happy to have made.

The point here is not to overlook opportunities to do what you need to (like look for a new job) but to celebrate life's twists and turns. Like the potter's wheel, when life twirls out quite a whirl, keep moving with it. While on the potter's wheel, we never really know how the heavenly Father will use life's revolutions to shape us. Seek purpose in each situation. Embrace each turn. Possess a purpose seeker's mentality.

DATE WITH DESTINY

Our purpose unfolds as we experience life's turns and uncertainties. Forrest Gump, the simple-minded character played by Tom Hanks, who is still one of my all-time movie favorites, said, "I do not know if we have a destiny, or do we just float around like a gentle breeze? Maybe it just happens all at the same time." I admire how Forrest withstood complex life issues such as self-acceptance, love and commitment, and the death of loved ones, while steadily moving forward. He was seemingly unscathed by any of those circumstances.

"Steady does it" summed up each of Forrest's life transitions, from enlistment in the Armed Forces to spontaneous cross-country trekking, for who knows what reason—and Ping-Pong championships for which he gained celebrity. Who can forget the Ping-Pong games? Priceless. Forrest did a whole lot of ordinary living, producing extraordinary outcomes, in a short amount of time. Take note.

Maybe one's destiny does unfold while doing the ordinary. Without even noticing, destiny just happens as life happens, without much thought. I am not suggesting that we should live passively, but could the unfolding of our destiny be as effortless as the "gentle breeze" Forrest Gump reminds us about?

Problems arise when we overlook the simple delight in living to the fullest now. Having our preconceived plan or notions for how things should go, without regard for the time it takes us to process through experiences, most of us are left plain-ol' frustrated. Wanting to be somewhere else except in the present. We've all been there. Respect the process. Will you?

Preparation serves as a vital part in discovering our purpose. As Forrest's longtime love, Jenny, returned to him, with the news of her pregnancy with his child, and dying suddenly, who would have ever guessed that his life's purpose included becoming a loving father? His son would not have had a known living parent, had it not been for Forrest's unconditional love for Jenny and his commitment to keep his promises.

Could all of his experiences, rejection, loss, and his own bout with disability have prepared him for what he was ultimately destined to become, what he had always desired? Maybe the sum of all Forrest's experiences had actually prepared him for what he had been waiting for all his life.

Purposeful Connections

Have you ever come across someone, and within minutes of casually conversing, it seemed as if you had known him or her ages before? Have you ever had an encounter like this one while at the grocer? At your child's soccer practices? While standing in line at the Department of Motor Vehicle Services? Think back to a time when meeting a stranger felt more like a divine connection of sorts. Why is this so?

Here is one view. Revealed within the contexts of relationships is an untapped reality of our extraordinary selves. Let me reiterate. We see who we can be through other people. On the other hand, we see our own shortcomings expressed through the irritating motivations of others. Watch it! We will address the latter in other chapters.

Words like destiny, plight, and yes, purpose should be viewed not through a lens of mysticism but rather as the coming together of seemingly random events to produce tangible and objective outcomes. In other words, should we endeavor to follow His plan? The path we take, the people we meet, and the outcomes we face may not all make sense now, but in the end, there be will something worth talking about! Knowing that is exciting, isn't it?

How It All Comes Together

For those who have concerns about how all this purpose stuff will come together, rest assured in knowing that as we connect ourselves to our God-preordained purposes, our hearts will align with His plan. Even powerful kings are subject to the plans of God. Proverbs 21:1 states, "The king's heart is in the hand of the LORD; He directs it like a watercourse wherever he pleases."

Since God is the Creator of one's purpose, remember, "purpose," then, is at the seat of God's own authority. Isaiah 46:11 illustrated this point perfectly: "Yes, I have spoken, and I will bring it to pass; I have purposed it, and I will do it." It is God's pleasure to ensure, with precision, its completion. That means every turn we take, every educational pursuit made or sisterhood circle joined all align to bring about God's desired plan for us. The key here is submitting to the plan. Shown through scripture, Isaiah 45:9, we see the sovereignty of God's hand in the selection of Cyrus as a powerful leader, carefully fashioned by our Maker:

> Woe to him who quarrels with his Maker, to him who is
> but a potsherd among the potsherds on the ground. Does
> the clay say to the potter, 'What are you making?' Does
> your work say, 'He has no hands'?

I discussed in earlier chapters how all experiences, both good and bad, make for your God-ordained purposes, even the people you encounter. Others often mirror your experiences, unrealized potential, and unfortunately, without a doubt, your need for recourse.

While discussing divine encounters, it is clear that no mysticism is being suggested here, nor is it meant to amplify the meaning of each encounter. After all, ordinary experiences like these are certainly relatable to the average person, but nothing special is said about them.

POTTER'S WHEEL REFLECTIONS

I like chocolates because it's the perfect excuse for bingeing on something sweet while boasting of quasi-health benefits (dark chocolate's antioxidants). I also agree with Forrest. Life is like a box of chocolates; "you never really know what you are going to get." Like chocolates, life presents opportunities to savor each moment as if the next is going to be even sweeter than the last. You really don't know for sure, but isn't life sweet anyway? It gets sweeter the more you delve into uncharted territory (a hopeful bite into another bit to discover a wonderful new flavor and texture). And what great joy you can experience during this process!

FRUIT OF THE SPIRIT CHECK: JOY

> Let us fix our eyes on Jesus, the author and perfecter of our faith, who for the joy set before him endured the cross, scorning its shame, and sat down at the right hand of the throne of God. (Hebrews 12:2)

Sweet chocolate life is sweet simply because you are granted freedom to experience life to the fullest extent God's laws allow! It doesn't really matter whether "delectable" experiences agree with the taste buds. Pain and disappointment quickly resolve as triumph and victory rally on your behalf to end the cycle of what is not truth, paving a way for what is. Your past washes and becomes the now, and the now forges new perspectives. You took some risks, learned a little more, broadened your perspective, revamped your personal mission statement, and grew more graceful. Hopefully, you'll richly experience all the chocolaty sweetness life has to offer.

It's Your Turn

Okay, chapter 5 is short and sweet and drives home the point that despite the certainty of uncertainty in our pursuit of purpose, we can have joy. As a matter of fact, joy—different from glee or happiness—is a hard-won fruit of the Spirit. Those who have cultivated joy must fight to protect its vitality. More than a pleasant disposition, joy's presence can be, simultaneously, a powerful weapon that transforms hopelessness and despair and a pesky irritant, a constant reminder to the joyless that, without it, _____ . (You fill in the blank.) Make no excuses; offer no explanation when joy overflows from within. Just say, "Hmmm, joy of the Lord. I fought for this one."

This time we'll do a confession instead of a prayer. Say it with boldness. Say it will power.

CONFESSION FOR JOY-FILLED PURPOSE

I Endeavor To:

1. Laugh, love, and inspire with new freedom never before experienced
2. Walk in new awareness of God's immense love for me, His chosen
3. Embrace God's love through others He has positioned in my path
4. Have fun without excuse, just because I can
5. Awaken to a new level, the awareness of my inherent kingship

In closing, I, (insert your name here), decree all these things in the life of (insert your name here), in line with the will of God for my life, and as God's Word declared before the foundation of the earth. Amen.

CHAPTER 6

POT BELLY

Purposeful Women
Await the Coming of God's Promises

If it isn't so
But God's word declared it is
It must become
It must become
Just what He said
Oh, oh, yes it will
It must become just what He said.

Ponder God's Promise

I embrace all things creative, even songwriting. Writing and singing not because this is for me mere craft; it is, rather, an outlet for declaring hope in tough places, encouragement to offset sometime-wariness, and awaiting promises when there's no confirmation of God's movement. Nevertheless, I know He is moving on my behalf, despite what it looks like. Having faith, this is why I sing God's promises. God likes it when I give back to Him the words He has already spoken. God likes me. He likes you too. Do you know and believe that?

FRUIT OF THE SPIRIT CHECK: FAITHFULNESS

O Lord, thou art my God; I will exalt thee, I will praise thy name; for thou hast done wonderful things; thy counsels of old are faithfulness and truth. (Isaiah 25:1)

I Sing Because I'm Happy

Celebratory singing is easy. Things are good. I have joy; therefore, I sing. That's intuitive, right? However, singing when you're joyful but awaiting fulfillment of a promise, well, that's divine. It takes God to find joy when all seems held up, but instead of losing hope, fan the flames of your heart's song. Find your Monday-through-Sunday heart song. Start singing it now!

Mary's Promise

I think Mary, mother of Jesus, could relate to what I'm speaking of in this chapter, as she awaited God's promise. Not really big on retelling Bible narratives, I proceed with caution in stating that no one on earth could have possibly felt like Mary, a virgin, who was stirred by an angel when told she would carry this never-before-experienced miracle for mankind. Pregnant, virgin, and God did that … hmmm. Now that's interesting. Bet that got the townspeople talking!

On a forced journey to Bethlehem, Mary and Joseph traveled in response to Caesar's required enrollment in a universal census. There was just one thing: everyone had to reside in his or her family birthplace to be counted. The problem was, both Mary and Joseph lived in Nazareth. Their hometown was Bethlehem. Did Caesar's decree really provoke this seventy-mile journey from Nazareth to Bethlehem? In the natural, yes, but God's hand was at work behind the scenes to bring about His plan through Caesar. Caesar was the conduit. Prophecy revealed seven hundred years earlier that Jesus's birthplace must be Bethlehem, period and end of discussion. They had to get there!

Therefore, God orchestrated the coming together of circumstances to align the words previously spoken by the prophets. Whatever it took, even a seemingly senseless decree from the mean old ruler, Augustus Caesar, was what God would use to bring about His proclamation. Remember, "Render unto Caesar what is Caesar's" (Matthew 22:15–22).

In another response to taxation, Jesus, in His adulthood, pulled coins from the mouth of a fish to cover taxes owed (Matthew 17:24–27). No need to consult Houdini for magic; Jesus is the man!

Birthing Promise

Flash back about thirty years, and we see this taxation bit come up again. This time, Jesus was a few days from being born, as Mary and Joseph traveled to their hometown to be counted in a census. Imagine how pregnant Mary must have felt: exhausted, irritable, and wondering why that donkey could not go any faster. "Oh, my swollen ankles, my aching back!" Traveling in the cold to Bethlehem, all for what—to be counted for census tax? Yes, but more importantly, traveling the road to Bethlehem fulfilling God's Word that the King of kings must be born there. After all, He was God's eternal promise to humanity.

Can you imagine that? What I do know is Jesus's immaculate conception and virgin birth tricked biological science as well as thwarted one man's attempt to squelch the birth of the soon-coming King. Not even King Herod could stop the fulfillment of a prophetic word and the aligning of specific circumstances to ensure protection of Jesus's purpose on earth. "Kill all the male children under two years old!" Herod decreed. Oops! Too late. Baby Jesus was not there as scheduled. God's plan intervened—again.

I believe Mary turned a deaf ear to all that was taking place around her; she had to, all the while possessing the kind of faith she (and no one else) had ever before exercised. Mary just believed. She pondered what everyone was saying of the future impact of her son's life, not swayed by any of it. Pondering what the angel had spoken, Mary wholeheartedly believed God. Can I get some of that kind of faith? Can I get it right now?

Faith is present when there is no other confirmation. Isn't that what faith is, anyway, believing without seeing? The only thing in the center of hope is faith itself. In other words, the very thing we use to believe God's Word depends on the thing that has no confirming evidence that it exists at all. Back to square one. "Faith is the substance of things hoped for, the evidence of things not seen" (Hebrews 11:1). Mary, the mother of Jesus, could write this book. So could some of you.

God Is the Promise Giver

Some of you today believe God for the extraordinary. The reality is this: more than any Bible story could illustrate, life is filled with opportunities to lose hope. Don't do it! Believing for the extraordinary requires extraordinary faith. I believe and come into agreement with you for divine fulfillment of God's promises for your life.

For Mary, it all seemed to begin with a word from God sent through an angel. However, for God, it began before time itself, confirming what was established prior through a seven-hundred-year-old prophecy. With the same detail and accuracy, God desires to bring to pass all (that means everything) things in line with your purpose. Adjusting circumstances in alignment with His plan, God has the all-consuming desire to fulfill His word, regardless of how it appears to us from a natural perspective!

> If it isn't so but God's word declared it is, it must become just what He said.

Know that His plan, not yours or mine, is far greater than what we could ever hope. Obedience to His way of bringing our purpose about unlocks the unknown but already divinely sowed desires of our heart. God put them there. Obedience is the key.

The will of God must be done in your life! Therefore, ponder promises for business opportunities. Ponder promises for true love and family. Ponder promises of health, wellness, and joy. Ponder promises for financial abundance. Ponder treasured promises only God could have placed in your heart. No matter what route you take to get to it, do it. Do it now! Do not depend on getting confirmation that He spoke to you. You may not get this. Just have faith.

> And Jesus answering saith unto them, Have faith in God. For verily I say unto you, That whosoever shall say unto this mountain, Be thou removed, and be thou cast into the sea; and shall not doubt in his heart, but shall believe that those things which he saith shall come to pass; he shall have whatsoever he saith. (Mark 11:22–23)

Move in the last thing He spoke to you. Hold it close to your heart like Mary did.

POT BELLY REFLECTIONS

As chapter 6 illustrates, submitting to faithfulness is the most critical part of the equation to "walk in purpose," and yes, there are many parts true purpose seekers enthusiastically seek out. You are faithful not only for the strength to endure the journey, but you also possess faith in God for His faithfulness in entrusting you to carry out your part.

FRUIT OF THE SPIRIT CHECK: FAITHFULNESS

> O Lord, thou art my God; I will exalt thee, I will praise thy name; for thou hast done wonderful things; thy counsels of old are faithfulness and truth. (Isaiah 25:1)

It's Your Turn

Reflect on the following questions: Do you really love God? Do you believe God? Do you trust God? Does it seem to be your time to experience God's promises? Then go after the big "it" with boldness! His Word said it. Do you believe it? If so, you move with confidence. Okay?

How Do You Begin Believing for God's Promises?

1. First, seek God in prayer concerning your life, desires, and purpose.
2. Believe that God wants to speak to you concerning your life.
3. Take authority over and purify any desires outside of God's will.
4. Repent to God about any unwillingness you may have expressed.
5. Exercise your faith; locate scripture to confirm only what He spoke to you.
6. Remember to give milestone testimonies to strengthen your faith.
7. Finally, wait, wait—and wait some more.
8. Watch God align circumstances to work on your behalf!

PRAYER FOR FAITH PERSPECTIVE

Father, sometimes the issues of life present themselves as insurmountable obstacles. I know You are a big God, guiding my destiny through Your strong hands with greater certainty than any issue I can concern myself with. Through every turn, I thank You, God, for giving me a new perspective, for the ability to see things through your eyes, for the fortitude to pursue purpose wide eyed with expectation, and for the faith to know that everything works together for my good. Amen.

CHAPTER 7

POTHOLE

PURGE

Purposeful Women
Joyfully Glean Wisdom from Life's Hard Knocks

The stage darkens as streams of light sneak between gathers where stage curtains meet. Play actors align themselves for the performance of a lifetime. This performance is not really one at all; rather, it is an account of their real-life experiences, hardly sensational enough to be fiction. Everyone has his or her story to tell, a story of hope and happiness, despair and disappointment.

FRUIT OF THE SPIRIT CHECK: LOVE

Charity suffereth long, [and] is kind; charity envieth not; charity vaunteth not itself, is not puffed up, Doth not behave itself unseemly, seeketh not her own, is not easily provoked, thinketh no evil; Rejoiceth not in iniquity, but rejoiceth in the truth; Beareth all things, believeth all things, hopeth all things, endureth all things. Charity never faileth: but whether [there be] prophecies, they shall fail; whether [there be] tongues, they shall cease; whether [there be] knowledge, it shall vanish away. (1 Corinthians 13:4–8)

That's life. Good endings make it easier for most to forget about the bumpy road traveled to greatness. Greatness costs a pretty penny or two, a cost well worth the investment. In some cases, the road to greatness often costs people their lives. Few women can order the path they must travel to fulfill their purpose. Sometimes it's a walk of blind faith. One thing we know for sure is there are plenty of life "potholes" to navigate. How we do this determines what story we tell.

Even though these stories are triumphant, they reflect a reality for many women, perhaps causing discomfort until a certain uplifting ending balances the bumpy road each character recounts in her monologue. Audience members begin to see that the actors' stories bear likeness to their own life experiences. Life is a series of experiences, some good, some bad. It's not how you start that counts. God rewards finishers, those who overcome.

Overcome Adversity

Do it with confidence. Your destiny depends on it, one pothole at a time.

Stage curtains slowly part. Silence fills the auditorium as the first actor approaches center stage. The first actor motions with graceful movement as she speaks with resounding voice, a testimony of strength. She recounts the kind of endurance most women of her time rarely knew but longed to embrace.

"I am Joan of Arc," proclaims the young woman, clad in traditional male clothing, her curly brown locks tucked under a hat that resembles cognac-colored silk ribbons. Queen Esther's birth parents, killed in a radical effort to annihilate Jewish people, left her in the care of an aunt and uncle. Jesus' mother Mary hid in seclusion her bulging belly; she had no husband and rumors spread about her claim to have conceived a son, the Messiah, while still a virgin.

Imagine for a moment what it took each woman to accomplish the task set before her. How does a life filled with rejection wear upon a person, feeling abandoned and not really fitting in? What does it feel like to be driven by a cause few could understand and even fewer possess the discernment to sense its urgency? Each woman did her God-assigned task while disappointed, rejected, unsupported, and certainly afraid. They moved forward anyway.

Then there's Hannah. She must have experienced feelings of worthlessness, as she was barren and faced daily ridicule by Peninnah, the most fertile half of the wife pair to husband Elkanah. Even today, barrenness can result in emotional turmoil. At this time in history, imagine how failing to produce children affected women like Hannah. Women married to have children and to care for their husbands. There weren't many alternatives at that time. Women were the family lifeline, and those producing sons were most favored.

Elkanah, Hannah's husband, had no idea what grieved Hannah so and had no way to heal her pain. In an attempt to reconcile the situation, Elkanah reassured Hannah his placement in her life meant more to him than ten sons (1 Samuel 1:8). Although people's attempts to alleviate our pain are often well-intended, they can sometimes fall short of patronizing us. Sweet and enduring, for sure, his reassurances only made matters worse. Hannah fell deeper into sorrow, grief, and depression until pleading with God to give her a son while promising to dedicate him for the Lord's use.

Even worse, sometimes male relatives and friends attempt with such sincerity to bring comfort but simply cannot relate, touch, or heal the pain women experience although they have good intentions. Women often seek out men to restore them back to wholeness but become only more disappointed, confused, and overburdened.

Saying Peninnah was mean, cruel, or evil for treating Hannah so badly is warranted, and that might be putting it mildly, but even in Hannah's pain, God had a wonderful plan in the works. God remembered Hannah's plea, and Hannah kept her promise. Samuel, the son of the once-barren Hannah, became a priest and a mighty war advisor.

I've always wondered about "the promise" that's at the end of the disappointment and pain we experience. You've heard it all before, the "hardships make good character" motif. I hear of those triumphant stories. You know them too—the endless testimonies of how women made lemonade from life's lemon experiences. I had constructed my own great scenario summing up what it all meant to have overcome hurtful situations, people's judgments, and my bout to seek forgiveness, self-forgiveness. Forgiving others seems the toughest to overcome.

Then there's the emptiness we feel after loss—loss of friendships because of brewing discord that one day erupts into irreparable damage. I, like you, know that God is always in control, even during hardships, but sometimes it's hard to see past what's staring us in the face. You know the saying "Can't see the forest for the trees." What's the point of seeing the message behind the madness? Harold S. Kushner, author of The Lord Is My Shepherd, explained it well:

> If there are empty spaces in your life, dreams that never came true, people who were there but are gone now, the purpose of those empty spaces is not to frustrate you or to brand you a loser. The empty space may be there to give you room to grow, to dream to yearn, and to teach you to appreciate what you have because it may not have been there yesterday and may not be there tomorrow. (p. 36)

Seek Freedom from Hurt

Depending on God's healing power essentially pulls us out of pothole experiences, propelling us forward on the road to destiny. Although women can understand the pain of other women, only God's supernatural love can heal them, making them whole. That's the plan, God's plan for your life, wholeness. Keep moving forward.

> The LORD is close to the brokenhearted and saves those who are crushed in spirit. (Psalm 34:18)

Today, women grapple with emotional distress stemming from past hurtful situations. Move forward anyway, knowing that in the process of fulfilling what you were born to do on this earth, you will not only accomplish but do so with a healed heart and healthy emotions. God establishes and protects your purpose, overseeing it vigilantly like each step taken toward your destiny. He also promises to restore healed hearts to those who have been broken along the way. It's a promise.

Supernatural Love for the Wounded Heart

Consider healthier options to heal yourself. You simply cannot keep revisiting every detail of the final meltdown, hoping to see where you went wrong; nor can you keep shifting blame to the other person or seek revenge. These methods of coping are simply poor substitutes to healing and become somewhat of a rehearsal for a mythical blockbuster entitled "Mental Torture." Where does it end? Often, efforts to fix situations may appear noble at the onset but upon execution, only make matters worse. We have all been there. You owe it to yourself to try a different approach to freeing yourself from guilt, shame, and false responsibility for the role you played in an unhealthy relationship, bad business decision, or past life of abuse. Seek supernatural healing for your wounded heart.

It's true. If someone hurts you, the Holy Spirit can create supernatural love in your heart. Do you remember your last argument with a close friend, when misspoken words deeply hurt your feelings, seemingly beyond repair or apology? Do you recall a young man who deceptively smeared your reputation merely because he wanted more out the relationship than you did? Is that memory of the woman who worked as your personal assistant and forged checks against your company without remorse and with a less-than-noble reason still hurting you? Now, really think about this one. Have you encountered mean church people? Enough said. Exchanges like these ultimately end relationships and can hurt you badly.

> You cannot amputate your (painful) history from your destiny … you cannot become the person who God is going to make you without [it]. He wants to take that part and make it your redemptive history. (Beth Moore, Esther: Being a Woman Is Hard Work, Session 1)

Often, contentious, strife-filled interactions are more than simple personality clashes due to miscommunication. Instead, destructive coping mechanisms directed toward others leave those on the receiving end wondering how they missed the loaded cannon aimed directly at them.

Emotional woundedness attempts to block purpose. If you challenge this assumption, then simply ponder for a moment how much time you spend rehearsing past hurt.

Understand the adversary's tactics to keep you wounded. The adversary also knows that if you keep your focus on your shortcomings, embracing a wounded awareness, you become distracted and may abort or partially fulfill your destiny; it's highly probable there will be a stream of wounded people you will have infected on your way "to the top."

I know the old adage and so do you: "Hurt people hurt people." Others are just plain mean, well, just because. Nevertheless, I am one who never discounts the influence of supernatural evil upon human behavior. The adversary is real, and he has a kingdom of darkness with stratagems as sophisticated as the kingdom of heaven. He, in fact, originally came from heaven, so where do you think he learned the model for his swanky operations? He stole from heaven's plan for a divine kingdom order and perverted it. He's a thief!

> The thief cometh not, but for to steal, and to kill, and to destroy: I am come that they might have life, and that they might have it more abundantly. (John 10:10)

The same way God strategically planned every blessing, promotion, and spiritual growth stage, likewise, the adversary mapped out a counterattack against the promises God has for you. Keep silent on this if you want. Acknowledging that a supernatural world exists means we either capitalize on our God-given authority to war for our destiny or allow our inheritances to slip away as our eyes close in slumber. Wake up! Know the adversary's tactics to keep you wounded; he too, like God, has a plan for your life.

> He heals the brokenhearted and binds up their wounds."
> (Psalm 147:3)

Let's face it: we cannot blame everything on the devil. Jesus already defeated him on Calvary; he can only work with what is already in us. Given the perfect crack or crevice in our frail human foundation, almost anything can seep through, put pressure on our weaknesses, and then we'll begin acting things out. Insecurity, jealousy, anger, and pride can manifest during these times. Even Jesus knows humans are but mere clay to God, subject to err, so He employs the Holy Spirit, empowering us to overcome these temptations.

Our frail humanity should make us grateful for God's grace. Without this awareness, our humanity can work against us as well, if we allow weakness to guide our interaction with others. Woundedness is never an excuse for not carrying out God's purpose for your life. Locate in the scripture the many servants of the Lord who, despite hurtful realities, carried out God's will. Undoubtedly, God desires supernatural healing for all of us, but the proverbial "thorn in the flesh" can serve to catapult us into the very place God has ordained. There are no excuses. God is more concerned about how we end a journey than what happens in the middle of the expedition. Go on and move forward!

> For I know the thoughts that I think toward you, saith the LORD, thoughts of peace, and not of evil, to give you an expected end. (Jeremiah 29:11)

Wounded Hearts Are Extremely Self-Protective

The wounded heart needs protection at all times, and unfortunately, the protective parts of our personality can employ hostility. For example, to cover up feelings of fear, shame, or rejection, hostility or bitterness may enter in, making it difficult for others to deal with us, and we them. The natural mechanisms we lack to handle conflict are often replaced with defensiveness that forms to cover up a wounded heart. Our desire for purposeful living must compete for space with the impression that past hurt leaves upon the heart, shaping our most intimate relationships with those who love us most. Coloring each interaction, broken-heartedness can even skew our impression of another person's good intent.

> If the Son therefore shall make you free, ye shall be free indeed. (John 8:36)

Finally Free!

No manner of evil that comes to take you off course can ever take away the fact that through the blood of Jesus, supernatural love is available to every wounded heart! I know what the experts say; however, the reasons you hurt in the first place—childhood hang-ups, for example—are but mere facts, the circumstances influencing our behaviors. The truth comes by knowing this: you have power over how hurtful circumstances affect you. A wounded heart can heal supernaturally. Not on your own, but with the Lord's intervention, dedicated time, and a large mirror image of your true selves, you will all walk in freedom from heart wounds.

Know the truth. Supernatural love can fix the wounded heart. Healing from past hurt begins with getting the right perspective, God's perspective. Your destiny depends on it: love yourself and others through God's eyes. God sees us through Jesus. Therefore, every pitfall we make He covers through the blood of His Son. Every mistake made, trial overcome, yes, Jesus already bore the sting of failure, hurt, and disappointment, so we may walk in freedom from guilt and shame! Forgive yourself; forgive others. Ask God to heal you.

It's okay to follow God's plan for your life and be normal despite a painful and less-than-perfect present—really, it is. So, when life gets "real stupid" on you and your loved ones begin resembling characters right out of Very Scary Movie, relax. Love God. Dig deep down to that place inside you where you find your resolve. Connect with your heart song. Move forward and sing; walk and sing. Skip if you must, but never ever stop moving—and, of course, never stop being normal, ever. No matter how scary life (or people) get!

You might be asking at this point in the chapter, "How exactly do I make sure I do not get stuck in a web of unforgiveness?" While there's no surefire formula to avoiding insult, hurt, and betrayal—after all, life simply happens—rest assured in knowing that signposts pointing toward the road to freedom after hurt are clearly marked. Surely, every purpose seeker will frequent this road.

POTHOLE REFLECTIONS

Trust and receive God's love. Have balanced love for yourself. Extend love to others—in that order.

I remember the time a friend of mine bellowed, "Girl, you're a control freak!" For crying out loud! We were having ice cream at the local grab 'n' go parlor in our neighborhood. This was to be a decidedly lively and pleasant outing; no fist fights, please. How exactly do you transition from ecstatic laughter to this: "Yes, I will have a double scoop of strawberry cheesecake ice cream in a waffle cone, and by the way, I am a what? A control freak?"

According to her, I was a mistress of manic detail recall, and I do this to think my way out of potential emotional harm. If I could only figure out when, where, and how potential emotional turmoil might occur, then maybe I could avoid it: preemptive emotional bailout. Yep, that's me! She made certain, however, to detail the fact that controlling people was not my issue, but I was a control freak nonetheless.

Well, since she framed it like this, I was forced (convicted) to consider my own contribution to this chapter on healing or, better yet, rid myself of the residue left over from spending many years successfully overcoming woundedness. First, my friend was right (said in hushed tones). Second, I was fully aware that I do this to protect my heart.

Besides driving myself and those closest to me nuts, I only most recently discovered the hidden hurt of Ms. Control Freak, since I rarely had a bad case of nastiness, was never vindictive or callous but was certainly overly analytical about what could potentially go wrong in my personal relationships, and when it happened, I conveniently sneered, "See there. I figured that! I told you so. There, right there, evidence. Don't you see it?" But I love people! I really do.

It's Your Turn

Whether or not I love people is not really the question, is it? What do you think? I take it that most women reading this chapter, even I, have some level of empathy for others, can celebrate with and are moved with compassion for others when they hurt. Generally speaking, we behave lovingly toward others not only because it is a biblical commandment but also because we are in debt to do so out of moral responsibility, good character, and so on.

So, what really is the deal here? Here's the explanation worth pondering. Perhaps our sometimes failure in forgiveness and love is actually not depending on God's Word to affirm His love for us. How much more can we walk in freedom, knowing that we can love others freely? No matter the outcome, God has everything in control; He loves us unconditionally and is the true judge and vindicator of wrongdoing. Give it to God. Forgive. Move forward.

How Do I Begin?

1. Repent to God for allowing bitterness and resentment within you.
2. Forgive those who hurt you; make the decision to do it, now.
3. Do not nurse or rehearse the situation or curse persons involved.
4. Cover yourself with scriptural declarations.
5. Ask God to forgive you for blaming others.
6. Love others without personal expectations.
7. Depend on God's Word to affirm His love for you.
8. Confirm your true worth in relationships.
9. War for your destiny by making forgiveness a lifestyle.

DECLARATION FOR EMBRACING GOD'S LOVE

I declare today that I walk in complete newness of heart. Substituting nothing for the space that God created for loving Him alone, I, through faith, believe the best, hope the best, and pursue the best in line with His will for my life. Absolutely nothing can separate me from God's love. Not even my own inability to fully grasp God's intimate, (and without flaw) hot pursuit of me. As I allow the Holy Spirit to minister to me, I will shed layers of humanity, the "false self" my defense mechanisms have constructed in response to pain, that which hinders me from embracing my true identity in Jesus Christ; my inherent birthright, the divinity in me that begs to reveal my position in God's kingdom.

CHAPTER 8

PURIFY

POTTER'S KILN

Purposeful Women
Submit to the Refiner's Fire

People are like houses filled with fine china. There is just one thing: the exteriors of most people's houses desperately need repair. Shutters are often broken and painted an undesirable shade, and chipped bricks need replacement mortar. There are indeed some handsome houses out there, even the ones needing minor home improvement.

The frail state of houses can be used to represent the state of humanity. We all have places of brokenness or those ramshackle areas in our lives that need a touch-up here and there. However, if constructed as a house with "good bone structure" and a solid foundation, our sometimes-tattered state does not take away from our innate inner beauty. Remember, God creates all things wonderfully. Therefore, what makes "people houses" so wonderful is not superficial perfection; rather, it is the incredible valuable, the unique treasure found within.

FRUIT OF THE SPIRIT CHECK:
SELF-CONTROL

> But also for this very reason, giving all diligence, add to your faith virtue, to virtue knowledge, to knowledge self-control, to self-control perseverance, to perseverance godliness, to godliness brotherly kindness, and to brotherly kindness love. (2 Peter 1:5–7)

That's just one part of it. More than just brick and mortar, contained within our unique "dwellings" are some of the most coveted valuables, heirloom furnishings passed down through the generations. Think for a moment of this as a representation of dreams, purpose, gifts, skills, and talents. God gave us these to bring about His perfect will and purpose for our lives.

Whether or not our home furnishings qualify for Sotheby's, the most prestigious antique auction in the nation, does not matter because we all assign value by way of the heart. If it's Grandma's coffee table or a local flea-market find, one glance connects us to the memory or emotion evoked at that moment. Just as cherished family photographs capture fond memories much like those evoked from passed-down family trinkets, we cannot ever relive the experiences they evoke. Therefore, we should covet valuables inside our "houses" like God protects His purpose imprinted within us as unique spiritual inheritances. His image of us is assessed through the value of Jesus's sacrifice: perfection, completion, and certainly, a person of highest value.

Home Improvement

Grieved by what I see while driving through some less-fortunate neighborhoods, I am careful not to pass judgment against those who live there. I might be part of the minority on this. "There goes the neighborhood," most would say, squinty-eyed and sure they'd want no part in that neighborhood's Saturday garage sale or its residents. What's more noble than the pristine playground that lies centrally, marking the place where all neighborhood streets meet, and well-meaning families come together with little ones to take part in their version of American family values? The mantra of these suburban neighborhoods is this: a family that spends time together, stays together.

The dilapidated playground, unfortunately, presents the contradiction: swing sets with chains but no seats, monkey bars with missing rungs, decomposing baby diapers strewn across the soil, serving no apparent purpose other than to incubate germs, and tattered sneakers hanging over broken power lines, nasty and useless.

Family love without boundaries is no easy feat, but it is doable. Loving in unlovely circumstances is divine—well, actually pretty close to it. How do we focus on what is important? I often wrestle to find solace in believing that undesirable neighborhoods are only superficial representations of the people living in them. Contrary to what we may believe, people are often not as they appear but are full of potential that, when presented with good opportunities, will take advantage, rally, and produce outstanding resolve to overcome any undesired circumstance. The notion that potential plus opportunity equals tenacity, the will to become better in how you behave, believe, and present yourself to this world, means you are becoming refined versions, exactly who we were created to be in the beginning.

> God makes us into the person He desires for us to become when we are obedient to the small details of our life. (S. Truett Cathy, Chick-Fil-A Company)

The Woman in the Mirror

This chapter deals with tough areas we must confront concerning ourselves, exposing those often-hidden, maladapted parts of our personality attempting to hinder our walk in purpose. You know the saying, "Hidden things usually find the most inopportune moments to show up." What's hidden does become known eventually. Now that the light radiates on you, let's bypass modern psychology for a moment to hit the route to wholeness. Shall we begin?

What's hiding in you? Is it negative thinking patterns or wrong attitudes, pride or deception? Would you begin by asking the Lord to reveal to you those hidden things, preventing you from fully embracing the purpose God has for you? Ask Him to burn it away, like the potter's kiln does unfinished areas of a clay pot, anything that prevents you from being what God intended. Will you submit to His refining fire?

Have you ever made a particular statement, the same statement you make to all your friends and coworkers, and that statement said to another person caused an explosive anger eruption? You apologize profusely for the offense it may have caused, not knowing why this person was offended in the first place. We all have bad days, but when this sort of behavior becomes a permanent part of our character, it begins to represent the behavior most people come to know us as having.

Enough Already!

C'mon, ladies, let's be honest. Some people have the knack for getting on your last good nerve, that nerve reserved for sanity. It's amazing! In almost a rehearsal-like manner, they are able to whip up contempt in your blood as their sneak attack unfolds. You know, those folks who know exactly what to say to get your entire day thrown off kilter. How do they do this? Something about them pushes your buttons. You can literally feel your blood pressure rise as they give you that glance, that resounding "hello," sinister nod, and simultaneous smirk.

It's the same grocery cashier who, without fail, overrings your purchase every time and leaves you questioning, "Is it me?" It's the menacing coworker who steals credit for nearly every assignment your bosses put you two together to complete. Who has a sabotaging family member who ups the ante on drama for every Christmas holiday gathering? What joy did Cousin Joe get from making Grandma Mabel cry? What evil ploy makes you a target for such distractions?

Fiery verbal exchanges among women have become commonplace in this society. Unfortunately, "keeping it real" and "telling it like it is" somehow become the verbal rites of passage to strong, powerful, and in-control womanhood. Are you serious? What's even worse? Every time you let people get to you, they come to expect the same response from you, and you oblige them without much thought. It's almost a Pavlovian conditioned response, the way we women snap back, sneer at, and blast anyone for attempting to break us down.

Honestly, most people are being themselves with little regard to which person their normal actions might gravely affect. "This is just the way I am" becomes their mantra, yours too. The truth is, initially provoked or not, your response to others' actions is something that only you can control.

Ladies, you will find that cultivating self-control, one of nine fruits of the Spirit, will become a lifelong process as we work to overcome purpose-blocking works of the flesh: Works of the flesh, like blighted buildings, are as valueless cesspits. Who can find value in such corrupted spectacles? An embarrassment to any city, indeed, a condemned building filled with lead-based paint, at least bulldozes easily, and then rebuilds as a newer property. However, it's a shameful reminder to the body individually and corporately (The body of Christ) that cosmetic cover-ups are no less superficial than fresh paint covering lead-based types. Lead-based paint "poison," though hidden, still imposes the same grave effects on everyone exposed to it despite its much healthier cover, its presence still detectable. Likewise, works of the flesh carefully masked will eventually experience pressure to surface. In time, even the proverbial wolf in sheep's clothing exposes its nature bold and true.

> Masking true intent and motives lasts only for a season,
> "Ye shall know them by their fruits." (Proverbs 17:9)

Refine the house we construct called personality, so true beauty shines. Is it enough knowing how to act Christlike, without examining the motivation behind behaviors preventing us from becoming Christlike in our interactions with others. When we claim, "This is just the way I am, my personality," it serves only to hinder personal growth when introspection helps to uncover potential weaknesses that may keep us from moving forward. Examine which parts of your personality help or hinder your growth. Ask friends and family how you handle stressful situations. Only then will you take proactive steps to discovering ways out of the convoluted web of heartache you may have created for yourself and others.

Beauty in Simplicity

I take like life real simple. Like walking barefoot on grass in the summertime. Grass that spreads thick as quilted fabric and deep; the kind of grass that freshly painted toes could get lost in. Real simple. Then life-real simple meets me sitting "Indian style" and closed-eyed, hoping to catch a calm breeze. And with innocence of a child, I imagine God rallying the elements together to make the calm breeze just for me, at that moment, for that time. I am silly enough to believe life-simple results like calm breezes come at just the right time, just for me, but this is half-truth. It's only God's behind the scenes handiwork that brings resolve to such climatic complexity. But you must leave it to Him to work the details. Just focus on His Promise, You just keep keeping life real simple. OK?

Deborah and Gideon (John 4:7) kept it really simple, remaining faithful to their roles as "instruments of change" while God's sovereign hand moved upon circumstances. Deborah—judge, prophet, psalmist, and war strategist—was "partner in ministry" to the reluctantly supportive Barak, "not her husband Loadoa," but Barak, the man God asked to perform a very specific task. I use "reluctantly supportive" because when Deborah needed Barak to hear and obey God most, Barak got scared. Cowardice never wears well on any man, but this man agreed to God's terms with one condition: if Deborah did not go with him to war, Barak would refuse to go at all. Let's all say in unison, chicken!

No Conditions

What's interesting? It was too late, and slothful obedience was not good enough. Deborah warned Barak that "because you delayed in responding to this assignment, God will give a woman credit for this war victory" (Judges 4:9 paraphrased). Barak had to fight a battle he would not get credit for!

I Am This, but God Said That ...

What was real as Gideon faced the harsh reality of what God chose him to do? He carried out his destined assignment scared, uncertain, and insecure, but not without God confirming His will in Gideon's life plan. "If you said it, Lord, then show me a sign" (Judges 6:39). Gideon got the go-ahead, and like Deborah, what made him real, true to his God-ordained purpose, when he could have dwelt on the facts? Perspective—that's right, how he moved, reacted, behaved, and thought, despite sometimes feeling that the weight of life's circumstances rendered him incapable or unqualified to execute God's instructions.

"Keeping it real" was not defined by how accurately each person synopsized the details of his or her bleak circumstances, vocalized pain, or shared disappointment and frustration.

"I am the least of my father's children; my father who was an idolater," Gideon may have asserted.

Lord, why would you put me in the position to judge a nation, develop war stratagems, and confront a noble man about his disobedience to Your commands? I am just a woman; that's a man's work.

Knowing all the facts did not keep them from moving forward in truth. What's real? God said Deborah was this and Gideon was that. He meant what He said, and circumstances had to line up with His Word. I'm just saying!

Trust me—life for most is not a walk in the park, a stroll through a Georgia peach orchard, or a pretty picture viewed through rose-colored glasses. Life is simply not that perfect. Would someone please tell Pollyanna the truth? Don't get me wrong. Times get hard, really hard, nearly overwhelming for some. Venting sometimes becomes our only solace, but be careful. Words have creative power (Genesis 1). Asserting what is believed to be the truth often really isn't. Sometimes what we believe are mere facts masquerading as truth. There is a difference. Why give power to something that can only play bad copy to the genuine article?

"Well, I ain't trying to be fake, so I'm a' just keep it real. All right?"

"I'm just saying!"

These statements become the mantra of many "keeping-it-realers" as they set at liberty those captive emotional verbal tidbits that bolster their tabloid-worthy proclamations. "You would not believe what just happened to me!"

"Been there, done that, and received the award for Most Dramatic Presentation in a miniseries called *As My World Turns*." Gave my award back when I got a new perspective and saw a new reflection in the mirror I blamed for showing me what I thought was true. Now I see the reflection of Christ! So can you. Do you?

Reflecting Him

Look in the mirror. What do you see? Imagine your life wrapped in Christ's sacrificial love, His character, His purpose and will for your life. Is this hard to imagine? Yes? Then remove yourself from this image. Go on and do it! Doesn't this reflection change? It has to. Life in Christ means a life in total submission to His image for us, an image minus self-doubt, insecurity, fear, self-hatred, and all other forms of devaluation. It's a single image in the mirror, and the reflection of us with Him becomes not two but one. His image replaces ours!

> When Christ, who is our life, shall appear, then shall ye
> also appear with him in glory. (Colossians 3:4)

Christ is your real life. Not yet convinced? Do you feel like your life is comparable to walking on a moving sidewalk, like in airports? Like your life is on automatic pilot, unable to add to or take away from any experience, good or unfortunate? Life's more good than unfortunate, but you're no longer in control. Perfect. Submitting to your real life in Christ feels somewhat like this at first. It gets comfier as you trust Him more. There's one thing, though. Your destination is set, and the unfortunate is promised to work to benefit you. (All things work together!) (Romans 8:28)

What's more, imagine this: when there is evidence of His in dwelling in you, it will overflow, and others will witness it; then the spiritual and natural riches of all His glory will also become your glory! Share in Christ's plan, purpose, and will for your life by fully knowing what's real. He is! Got it? Get it! Go on, and find your real life in Christ, the real you God created you to be, reflecting His truth. Now, that's keeping it real. I'm just saying!

What Is *Not* Real?

- I am helpless to overcome family cycles.
- I cannot seem to move forward.
- The memory of my past still haunts me.
- I am fearful, inadequate, and cannot be alone.
- No one will ever love me like I need them to.

What Is Real?

"Your life is hid with Christ in God." (Colossians 3:3)

POTTER'S KILN REFLECTIONS

Whew! Chapter 8 is a tough one. If you have not figured it out yet, this book is not about learning to employ the proper skill set to draw the right opportunities, but its primary goal is assisting you in unlocking your extraordinary purpose, finding the pathway aligning your Godordained destiny. It is about working on you. Dying to old patterns of behavior that can hinder you from moving forward from mediocre existence to the extraordinary is necessary as you submit to God's plan of preparation.

Chapter 8 shows us what kind of attitudes and beliefs can hinder or block purpose on our destiny journey. As you examine these, reflect on ways you might avoid attitudes and behaviors preventing you from seeing the truth of the vastness of your purpose. I have identified six reflection points to aid in assessing your walk in purpose.

WALK IN PURPOSE CHECK

Check it out! Do you possess these perpetual promoters of kingdom purpose?

Do You Walk Out Purpose …?

1. Assertively
2. Without compromise
3. With a kingdom-centric view
4. As one who seeks God for direction
5. While working on your weaknesses

PRAYER FOR REVEALING MY LIFE HIDDEN IN CHRIST

Lord, please forgive me for giving power to words spoken over me, to beliefs I formed in opposition to my renewed nature in Christ, to behaviors that set in motion my character traits, to circumstances that colored my perspective, and to people I allowed to shape my perception of You, Your plan and purpose for my life. Today, I let go of it all. Everything that blocks me from seeing me the way You see me. Now reveal the hidden treasure within me, my real life, and the promise of all Christ's glory that comes with it. Amen.

CHAPTER 9

PRESENT

POT 'O' GOLD

Purposeful Women
Identify the Great Treasure of Being Uniquely You

If heaven is on earth, then I'm walking barefoot in the rose gold section! I am woman. Powder pink shimmer painted toenails or clear. And choosing to walk barefoot means, I'm free to embrace womanhood the way God intended: standing tall, bold, sure, and yes, barefoot as I walk. Walking this way means, I'm protected so I have no fear. "On rose gold?" you might ask. I say, "Why not" as long as I am walking, in heaven on earth—the place where I meet purpose for the first time, welcome her with grand expectation, take her guiding hand of wisdom, and trek along rose gold-laden paved roads called "my journey." I chose the rose gold section simply because this is where purpose and destiny will unite to celebrate my faith-filled triumphant walk in freedom as woman. Free to be "me." The "me" God intended me to be.

There's nothing more inspiring than a woman who knows what she wants and what it'll take to get it. It's downright contagious to be around her if she pursues her purpose as a humble woman of virtue! Authentic womanhood begins with discovering what makes your "inner fabulous" personal attributes so magnetic to others or what makes women of God stand out as unique. It's more than superficial glam or outward expressions of beauty that mark authentic womanhood.

Being pot 'o' gold is all about inner beauty, the kind of beauty only God's presence can radiate through us as we cultivate the fruit of goodness.

FRUIT OF THE SPIRIT CHECK: GOODNESS

> For ye were sometimes darkness, but now [are ye] light in the Lord: walk as children of light: For the fruit of the Spirit [is] in all goodness and righteousness and truth. (Ephesians 5:8–9)

CULTIVATING GOODNESS

For some women, relating to others through relationships is like breathing. It comes naturally and with little exertion. For everyone else, me included, maintaining positive relationships takes real work. Purposeful connection, on the other hand, in either instance, is a rare occurrence for most. Although we would think otherwise, divine connections occur not for our immediate personal gain but so that we may align ourselves one step closer to fulfilling a purpose God has established for His people. Imagine that!

God's purpose for our lives affects entities outside of us, though usually He funnels His work via the passion, experience, skills, and personality of a single person, group, or system. Following His plan positively affects many others in the process. This is completely like God, who is relational; His influence extends everywhere.

This leads me to this statement: women are life-givers, having tremendous creative power to speak life into others, especially other women, but I must question sometimes why some of us withhold the precious treasure within us, the ability to share, impart, encourage, and support other women. Nothing else can bankrupt our own self-esteem like withholding valuable love "deposits" to others. I mean, really! How can building up another take something from you?

> For this light within you produces only what is good and
> right and true. (Ephesians 5:9)

So, ladies, next time you're at Wal-Mart, and you see a well-put together sister, don't turn away. Make eye contact and smile. If she returns the same, say, "Hey, sis, you're the fire! And by the way, you're rocking those stilettos!" If you're at church, say, "The beauty of the Lord is upon you" (Psalm 90:17). Trust me; it's biblical. Speak life into others by allowing the goodness of the Lord to shine from within you. This chapter, "Pot 'o' Gold," is all about becoming the living, breathing extension of God, the authentic alpha women He intended you to be.

AUTHENTIC ALPHA WOMANHOOD

What is an alpha woman? Without having to offer a lengthy explanation, most would gather that the term "alpha" preceding the term "female" distinguishes specific qualities possessed by some women. Alpha (α) is the first letter of the Greek alphabet. Alpha also has its roots in many disciplines. For these, I will provide brief explanations.

- Astronomy: Alpha is the brightest or main star in a constellation. ("Bayer Designation")
- Biology: Alpha in the Animal Kingdom represents the highest ranking of its sex in a dominance hierarchy, for example, the alpha female. ("Alpha Ethnology")
- Chemistry: Alpha is the first position for a carbon atom in an organic molecule at which an atom or radical is substituted. ("Alpha and Beta Carbon")
- Business and Finance: Alpha is an excessive rate of return on a security or portfolio that is much higher than predicted by Capital

Asset Pricing Model (CAPM). An alpha of 1.0 means the fund outperformed the market 1.0 percent. ("Terms Alpha")

- Technology and Computing: Alpha, as in machine learning, is the degree to which a learning agent takes into account new information. ("Q-learning")
- Music: Alpha describes the name of the sixth tone in the model major scale (that in C), or the first tone of the minor scale. The second string of the violin is tuned to the A in the treble. ("Whole Tone Scale Staff")

Common themes connect the term "alpha" in each of the preceding disciplines. This noted, in social situations, "alpha female" describes the most prominent, talented, or aggressive person in a group. In dating, this term has been linked to very specific and often undesirable character and temperament traits. There is great power, however, in employing alpha mechanics to gain advantage over others, and sadly enough, it usually works, but not without severe consequences. These are tactics women use to get others to think they are the strongest, most powerful, and most sought after. In other words, it is a façade, an outward presentation we make to the world to manufacture the appearance of beauty, power, prestige, or likeability.

Authentic womanhood is evaluated quite differently in the kingdom of God. The godlike woman, instead, becomes dominant, bright, primary, and high ranking for the virtuous traits she possesses. People tune in to the "signal" of the alpha woman, wanting to be like her. Others desire to possess traits that will also make them the "lioness of the pack." Likewise, the term "queen bee" takes on quite a different meaning.

Alpha mechanics apply to both sexes. With the focus on different positions of authority, God created both sexes to possess authority, that is, in a specific area of influence. From this perspective, we can do away with confusion stemming from gender-based role assignments and relationship competitiveness that come when women have not yet identified the area where their authority lies. Naturally so, men having difficulty making a mark in their area of influence may find difficulty posturing as the leader God intended them to be long ago.

ALPHA WOMEN AND INTEGRITY

I've always wondered about integrity. People refer to it alongside its sister, character, with the same commonness as a southerner does good manners reflected by the gracious respect of the language used: please, thank you, yes ma'am, and yes sir.

"He or she has good character."

"She handled this situation with such integrity!"

> Our character…is an omen of our destiny, and the more integrity we have and keep, the simpler, and nobler that destiny is likely to be. (George Santayana)

Kingdom Integrity

> Strong's Concordance records 16 uses of words translated as "integrity" in the KJV Old Testament, and none in the KJV New Testament One view of integrity in a Christian context states: "The Christian vision of integrity suggests that personal authenticity entails living in accordance with personal convictions that are based on an understanding of God's purposes for creation, humankind and the person as a disciple of Jesus."

Integrity is uncommon. "Lacking nothing essential" defines what it is. As a house without a foundation cannot support a frame and a chair without screws and bolts isn't a chair at all but a pile of well-fashioned wood pieces unable to perform what it was created to do, the lack of integrity renders every talent or gifting useless in becoming who God intended.

Likewise, a life of integrity is the evidence or proof that you are qualified to progress through each stage of your purpose, completing each assignment. Complementing integrity, character represents a wooden chair's patina or outward finish. Character is how you show the world that, yes indeed, what you say, do, and think lines up with who you really are. Luckily, integrity keeps us this way.

What Does Goodness Have to Do with Integrity?

Having integrity isn't choosing the lesser of two evils. It's making the higher-ground change of direction, an excellent decision, behavior, action, or thought that leaves everyone wondering "What's the big deal, Goody-Goody?" The truth is that this projection of superficial goodness has nothing to do with integrity at all. Integrity is never about everyone else but always about you. You are the first domino leading the integrity chain reaction. The starting lineup marshaled behind integrity goes straight to the finish line. Integrity is all about y-o-u.

> For ye were sometimes darkness, but now [are ye] light in the Lord: walk as children of light: For the fruit of the Spirit [is] in all goodness and righteousness and truth. (Philippians 3:9)

Let Integrity Be Your Guide

Integrity is what makes alpha women a pot 'o' gold. It creates sound measured in kingdom decibels, not only gauged by what you do but also by what you give up. Integrity creates an inaudible sound but resounds nonetheless. Women of integrity will encounter many opportunities to practice and assess their integrity; however, in personal interactions, I like to think of integrity like this: "It's the barometer gauging what really warrants a response from you." Really? After all, as Meister Eckhart stated, "In silence man can most readily preserve his integrity."

Integrity Is ...

1. Confessing faults to people, knowing they didn't even notice and would love you anyway
2. Going to a spit-nasty coworker to apologize, even though you're not at fault
3. Continuing to volunteer in church after random gossip served to keep you away
4. Redefining your "walk in love" from being nice to heart-level sincerity backed by action

5. Depending on God to supply your needs, not people, jobs, or hope of the "next big thing"
6. Choosing to wait on God's choice for your mate if the one you're with is almost right
7. Deciding to walk in integrity, even when nobody is taking notice

Integrity Is Not …

What everyone else is doing, saying, thinking, and believing, only about you.

Short list? Precisely. It takes very little exertion to make this point. When you're caught in the middle of tough situations already in motion, integrity can become the standard-bearer's signal for a change in another direction.

POT 'O' GOLD REFLECTIONS

What does alpha mechanics look like? Jesus is the ultimate servant-leader, like our heavenly Father, who is the alpha originator. (We read in Revelation 22:13, "I am the Alpha and the Omega, the First and the Last, the Beginning and the End.") By virtue of creation, every person is "created in His image and likeness" (Genesis 1:27). Therefore, you are now empowered to capitalize on unique attributes comprising your inner fabulous, discovering which factors are waiting to be revealed in you. Yes, y-o-u, and you will not be hasty to say, "I have potential to hone my inner-fabulous factor and rush forward to grab my pot 'o' gold, the goodness of God's promises, at the end of the rainbow."

FRUIT OF THE SPIRIT CHECK: GOODNESS

For ye were sometimes darkness, but now [are ye] light in the Lord: walk as children of light: For the fruit of the Spirit [is] in all goodness and righteousness and truth (Ephesians 5:8–9).

It's Your Turn

Ladies, rest assured, God has it all worked out: His plan for your life, the methods He uses to get you there, and the people you will affect in the process. How cool is that? Every good time and bad time, every up and down, your personality and style and upbringing already fit perfectly into the plan of God. In fact, I would venture to say, God was waiting on someone just like you, so much so that He had you already factored in the equation far before Mom and Dad began to date! When in doubt, remember God's message, as the prophet Jeremiah proclaimed: "He knew me before I was formed in my mother's womb" (Jeremiah 29:11). Therefore, you are His original idea! Let's say it together: "I was God's original idea!"

With this in mind, you will also discover yourself asking to uncover which character traits define your "alpha mechanics" aptitude, the measure of authentic womanhood as God sees it.

ASSESSMENT FOR DISCOVERING MY ALPHA MECHANICS

1. Integrity: Do I buckle under pressure to do the right thing?
2. Purity: Do I live a life of physical and spiritual purity, pure thoughts and actions?
3. Strength: Can I submit to seemingly wrong or unfair instruction given by leadership, even if I know a better way?
4. Leadership: Do my decisions reflect well on me and others in front of other leaders and behind closed doors?
5. Courage: Do I cower in fear in the face of real or imagined offense, and can I be counted upon in the face of conflict?

You also cannot expect to have mastered all areas but should work toward perfecting character, which is an ongoing process, the way God intended it to be. Please do not stop here with these questions. Create your own list, and do not forget to assess yourself honestly. Ask friends to help you. How will you fare with alpha mechanics?

CHAPTER 10

PRESENT

VESSEL OF HONOR

Purposeful Women
Yield to Preparation as Vessels of Honor

Repeat after me, "I am a vessel of honor fit for the Master's use." Now, repeat it twice more. The last time, own it, like you believe it's real! This is real. Now that you believe it for sure, you might ask, "What makes me an honor vessel, and what does a pot have to do with pursuing my extraordinary purpose?" Honor vessels are what women become as we submit our lifestyles in sanctification, righteousness, and purity; your destiny depends on it.

> But in a great house there are not only vessels of gold and of silver, but also of wood and of earth; and some to honour, and some to dishonour. If a man therefore purge himself from these, he shall be a vessel unto honour,

sanctified, and meet for the master's use, [and] prepared unto every good work. (2 Timothy 2:20–21).

There's something about the "purity" message that puts people on guard. I understand why. The funny thing is this: few people disagree on this point. No one likes to be uncovered, put under a speculative microscope, and dissected by a list of misapplied scriptures, which quasi-spiritual surgeons themselves fail to follow. What is this purity "holier-than-thou" madness?

FRUIT OF THE SPIRIT CHECK: KINDNESS

We should live "in purity, understanding, patience and kindness; in the Holy Spirit and in sincere love; in truthful speech and in the power of God; with weapons of righteousness in the right hand and in the left" (2 Corinthians 6:6–7).

If I'm preaching to the choir, then call me the reluctant messenger and let me join you in the next song selection. Trust me, I am not the Holy Spirit patrol, searching here and there for any unsuspecting someone in violation of God's command to be pure. This clearly is backward thinking, as it angers the targets of such "holy roller" propaganda—the kinds of stuff secular tabloids are made of.

You've heard it all before: "Now, don't you go backsliding between Sundays! You hear me?" There are too many things other Christians can say and think about you as they pan for evidence to prosecute you on the merit of their perceived indiscretions of your actions. Will a too-short skirt hem on the front pew become Christian decorum violation number one? Give me a break! Then, those appearing to go soft on the purity message become key witnesses for the prosecution as they introduce new evidence that offers a balanced perspective. Not fair. Does it ever end?

As you well know, tangible evidence is only symptomatic festering of a much bigger problem. Me, you, we all have contributed in some form or another. Take a deeper look. Have you ever ignored blatant wrongdoing or participated in condemning judgment of another? Even if it was unintentional and without malice? Acknowledge it or not, judgment is different from correction, though people conveniently confuse the two. There's no mistaking. Loving correction heals people. Unsympathetic judgment of others' actions perpetuates their issue, leaving accusers at risk of falling into the same sin spoken.

Judgment is not the focus of this chapter. In the scriptures, we find God's verdict, and He has the definitive answer:

> But the LORD said unto Samuel, Look not on his countenance, or on the height of his stature; because I have refused him: for [the LORD seeth] not as man seeth; for man looketh on the outward appearance, but the LORD looketh on the heart. (1 Samuel 16:7 KJV)

Passionately pursuing your purpose is all about the heart. Evidence of lifestyle purity is not entirely cosmetic or measured superficially by what you (and others) think demonstrates the Christian walk. What is spiritual eventually produces outward confirmation of this transformation, but not always, if you're looking through your lens and not God's eyes—the life of Jesus.

When there is no outward evidence of who you really are, can the glory of God still radiate from within?

Keeping It Kosher

This leads me to tell the story of Rachel, a little girl I sat for while in graduate school at Emory University. Well, actually, there were three: Alexandra, Rachel, and Sarah. Rachel, the often-precocious middle child, was most impressionable and, as the theory goes, fought fiercely to maintain her reputation. She was five then and readying herself for kindergarten entrance testing at a prestigious Jewish preparatory school. That evening, I played nanny.

After bath time, I wandered my way around the enormous ranch on a basement to the room of Sarah, the youngest child, then on to Alexandra, the eldest. True to form, Alexandra's bedtime story time met me with bewilderment. As she had outgrown adult readings to her, Alexandra's room visits were usually brief, but they were made to see how far she might go to escape into magical fantasy, whilst scanning the pages of the latest Harry Potter book.

I often found her crouched on her knees, comforter pulled up to her head, and eyeglasses resting on the tip of her nose. Then there was the quick upturned-nose glance she'd give me as I peeked through at her.

"What?" she'd sneer at me, and then catching herself and reflecting, I could see her rehearsing in her head a suitable reply to her snap response as I stood there squinting back at her, shaking my head. Everything seemed very normal there, so I'd move to the next.

Sarah is the complete opposite of Rachel. Footloose and fancy free describes her, even on not-so-good days for a two-year-old. That's why she wasn't really a "terrible two" at all, not even close. She has the temperament of a hand puppet on a very happy hand. I can still see her curly, golden locks bobbing up and down as she shook the crib, almost ritualistically, each night I laid her down for the evening. This was simply her thing. Children have their thing. Alexandra's thing was to establish independence as she was maturing, and Rachel, well, finding her place in the big world, sometimes at any cost.

Hoodwinking, sweet manipulation, you name it—Rachel tried everything. Like the time I had forgotten which one of the two sinks was reserved for meats. This was clearly not kosher! Kosher: fit, proper, and acceptable. Rachel's pranks simply were not acceptable (but cute, nonetheless), as she got joy out of pulling my leg, finding any way she could to make me foul up kosher-keeping at mealtime.

"Rachel, now you knew better!" Bev, too, knew her daughter well. Like a grownup, I blamed my misdirected instructions to plop down the remains of a lovely Middle Eastern lamb dish Bev had prepared earlier on Rachel.

This was a big deal! Jewish households keeping kosher have a two sinks rule, one reserved for meat and another other for dairy and everything else. Rinsing dishes in the wrong sink can mean very little to Christians who do not observe this practice. However, to an assertive Jewess slash home engineer, things could get very complicated quickly. I was certain I would lose my nanny job over this one. I did not. Spared termination and given another chance to pay attention, I counted my blessings for this.

As it turned out, my stay abroad in Haifa, Israel, during a summer college internship should have prepared me well for kosher living. There were no motorized travels during Shabbat, which began at sundown Friday and ended at sundown Saturday. There were no cheeseburgers, ever, not even at McDonald's.

Keeping the Temple Holy

Often compared to a temple, the dinner table of Orthodox Jews observing kosher practices reflects spiritual purity. Religious tradition is undoubtedly paramount, as there are over twenty-six dietary laws devoted to kosher food preparation alone. However, the kosher tradition is born out of pure reverence for whole-body purity. After all, "Kashrut," the term for these dietary laws, comes from the Hebrew word meaning "fit" and "proper" and literally through scriptures, this way of life found significance in Jewish food tradition (Leviticus 11:43–44). It's the Jewish law or "halacha" that guided selection and preparation of certain foods.

Keeping a Pure Vessel

Jewish law also distinguishes differences between "tahor" (holiness) and "tamai" (defilement) in daily living. For example, in a holy temple, clean vessels of clay and golden pots housed the most acceptable offerings to God. Only pure vessels or animals were deemed proper for consumption. Likewise, discovering the connection between spirit and body is a matter of godly reverence.

> For I am the Lord your God; sanctify yourselves and be holy, for I am holy. (Leviticus 11:44)

Hayim Halevy Donin, author of To Be a Jew, offers explanations regarding the link between lifestyle and spiritual purity. He states, "Transference of this religious discipline to other areas is not guaranteed, but there is no denying the inherent" (Donin, 100). "An aspect of the broader requirements that Israel learn to 'distinguish between the unclean and the clean' not only in food, but in all areas of life the sexual, the moral, the ethical, the spiritual" (Ibid.).

The point here is not to advocate or oppose specific dietary practices or require strict adherence to food standards or challenge the basic tenets by which kosher practices form Jewish culture. This discussion means more. What is clearly shown here is God's original intent. You are like a human container or vessel created to honor God wholly, without constraint. Minimizing potential barriers to holistic worship is a kosher (acceptable) practice, even for disciples of Christ.

Spiritual purity is kosher. Offering this parallel helps paint a vibrant portrait of exactly what God intended for His kingdom placed inside of you, becoming vessels of honor fit for His use (Acts 9:15). This happens not through your quest for perfection but through submission; you become a woman who is a vessel of honor.

Preparation must precede "honor status." God desires all women to be vessels of honor. The call for integrity requires practice and empowerment, not perfection. You are this chosen vessel not because you've got it all together but because you practice what it takes to become an honor vessel. In this instance, practice does make permanent. There's more; God not only honors us as we submit our whole life to Him— mind, body, and spirit—but also commissions us as honorary carriers of His glory, His power, and His complete purpose. Ultimately, lifestyle purity positions us as "earthen" honor vessels (Acts 9:15), unlocks valuable treasure within us (2 Corinthians 4:7 KJV), and reveals our real life hidden in Christ (Colossians 3:1–3). When Christ, who is your whole life, is revealed to the world, you will share His glory (Colossians 3:3). It's His promise and purpose for our lives.

VESSEL OF HONOR REFLECTIONS

Our walk in purpose is worship. Today, God still highly regards purity as total-life worship among deeds honoring Him most. The same principles apply, except that Christ, rather than a burnt offering or unblemished pot, became the sacrificial Lamb of God, and by spiritual rights, we are joint heirs to God's promises. Taking the same position as Christ places believers in right standing with God. Believe that God does indeed have something very special for you. Pursue your promise with boldness as you walk in kingdom integrity.

FRUIT OF THE SPIRIT: KINDNESS

We should live "in purity, understanding, patience and kindness; in the Holy Spirit and in sincere love; in truthful speech and in the power of God; with weapons of righteousness in the right hand and in the left." (2 Corinthians 6:6–7)

It's Your Turn

Reflect on chapter 9, gathering all fruit of the spirit themes covered in these preceding chapters. Then read the following poem, "Potter's Refinement Project." How might the following quote relate to your walk in purpose, your quest for kingdom integrity? "Integrity combined with faithfulness is a powerful force and worthy of great respect" (Anonymous, 2003). How well does the poem bring together principles of wisdom gleaned from each chapter? Preparing for your purpose is a walk in kingdom integrity.

POTTER'S REFINEMENT PROJECT

Lacking nothing
necessary
Essentially all I need
To make His kingdom
Inside me
Radiate Glory
Worth more than a finely crafted
vessel Now, what's contained therein
Brings Him Honor

I am a vessel
Overflowing, not with issues,
but with sacrifice

Living, breathing, moving, and being
The Potter's Refinement Project
Shaping, firing, breaking and
remaking Over and over and over again
Then this overflowing
Became evidence uncovering
My Real Life found only in Jesus Christ
The Judgment overturned
There is no turning back

What is deemed pure and uncommon
In God's Eyes
Is Honorable Becoming
this Honor Vessel Through Jesus Christ
The Holy Spirit reminds
me I am fit for the Master's
use And I will name IT
This Overflow
kingdom
Integrity

(Edwards 2010)

BONUS CHAPTER

PURPOSEFULLY SINGLE
AND PREPARING

As a nine-year-old, I spent time investigating things, creating from whatever items my hands could grasp and my mother would allow. Anything requiring mixing, melting, drawing, and sewing or putting together, I loved. Not one for dolls or make-believe, instead, I filled my summers in secret. Secretly, I had prepared the next craft, song, or concoction to present to my mom. She had always encouraged my creativity; she also bought me dolls. I did not like dolls. They just sat there lifeless, doing nothing, except for the doll whose eyes blinked. I liked that. Sometimes one eye would delay a blink, stick, or not blink at all. Lifeless dolls are like this, unpredictable. While I appreciated these additions Mom made to my floor-to-ceiling doll shelf filled with Cabbage Patch Kids, "walking" dolls, life-sized stuffed animals, and yes, the blinking-eyes doll—hands-on activities most intrigued me.

My Barbie pool was just right for me. I could add water to it and create a real-life experience. I liked real life. Barbie actually floated in the mini-pool as her hair fanned into an impressive peacock-featherlike image, save the rainbow colors. (Who could forget Barbie's long blonde hair?) Unfortunately, Barbie and Ken did not fit in the pool together well at the same time. I bent Barbie's legs, so she could assume a seated position at the edge of the pool as Ken laid prostrate, head grazing one end of the pool, feet touching the other. Then it was Barbie's turn to take a dip; Ken looked on from the fence. (I propped him against the plastic fence.) His legs would not bend like Barbie's, so he just stood admiring her. Ken liked looking at Barbie.

Amid my handmade creations and swim time with Barbie and Ken, I became an avid daydreamer. I propped myself up on windowsills, as I peered into tree-crowded fields or common backyards. There, I dreamt about what I would become when I grew up, whom I would marry. I promise to goodness God would assure me in a most delicate manner, "I've got big things for you, little girl"; for this reason, I trusted Him and genuinely believed His gentle assurances. I knew God liked me then; I liked Him too. He still likes me today. From these first experiences, I have learned ways to keep Him liking me, uncovered new ways to please Him, created new experiences to find reasons for Him to like me even more.

Simple Things Matter

Simplicity teaches us. These true accounts of my childhood experiences reveal some practical, almost metaphoric, advice about relationships: Barbie is more flexible than Ken, and while sitting on windowsills, you will find God. Well, maybe. No seriously—in jest, I reveal an important principle for single women. Single women who are waiting on their Boaz appear more attractive as they actively pursue their purpose. Fanciful, childlike wonder uncovers passion that drives this pursuit. Encourage self-discovery without reservation. Discover purpose.

With this in mind, it becomes easier to put aside, if only temporarily, relationship how-to's and instead delve into an intimate relationship with the one who created relationships in the first place. After all, few men will ever notice women who wait idly for them to marry. Women on the move impress true men of God. Any man, for that matter, might be a bit leery to approach a woman unless she is busying herself in service, volunteer work, hobbies, education, or travel.

FOLLOW RUTH'S WAY

In Ruth 2:3 and 5, we read, "So Ruth went out the gather grain behind the harvesters … and it happened, she found herself working in a field that belonged to Boaz, the relative of her father-in-law, Elimelech." After greeting the field workers, Boaz commended them for their hard work, and then Boaz said, "Who is that young woman over there? To whom does she belong?" The first question that comes to mind is, "What about Ruth that stood out"? Boaz was a very wealthy man, with many workers tending his fields. I am sure he noticed many of them, but apparently, Ruth was in the right position to catch Boaz's attention, and she did this as she worked!

Ruth also worked quite impressively. We read further in Ruth 2:7 the field supervisor's impression of Ruth's industriousness: "She asked me this morning if she could gather grain behind the harvesters. She has been hard at work ever since, except for a few moments' rest in the shelter." Did you grasp that? Ruth asked the supervisor for a position out of plan view behind the workers. Discretion, Ruth's way, appears to reflect the kind of womanly character God expects of every single woman. Here, the notion of "gleaning in the field" takes on quite a different meaning. Discretion goes a long way in a world filled with blatant disregard for the classy women, and godly character and timing. Single women, shall we consider Ruth's example?

When Will My Time Come?

Single women everywhere wonder when their time will come. Without having to go into minute detail, most women know to what I am referring. Toss the rice, jump the broom, crack the glass, meet the king, just like Esther of Susa. Whatever we choose to call this vitally important cultural tradition, and whichever cultural symbols suit our preferences, it all means the same: getting married. For some, this whole ordeal can be exhausting.

I have heard stories from young women everywhere. "I have been planning my wedding ever since I was ten years old." I often questioned, was she serious? For other women, divine unction guides their preferences.

"I just know I will marry rich, be a pastor's wife. The Lord told me he is the one!" Yet, in other fanciful "wishions" (wishes plus visions), some women with twisted thinking patiently await the breakup-stage scandal leading to the separation or even death of the girlfriend or spouse of the man whom they think they were supposed to marry. Give me a break! As I write, I wage a holy assault against this deceptive mind-set. Stop that now! Be real with yourself. Is this really what you want? Just be normal.

What a Woman Wants—Everything and That Too!

I recall a quote by Sigmund Freud in his assessment of the woman: "The great question …, which I have not been able to answer … is,

'What … does a woman want?" With simplicity, Freud surmises an otherwise complex phenomenon: the care with which women must balance their wants, needs, and desires. A very careful balance marks the purposefully single woman. What a conundrum, and do not think Freud was referring to the single women only!

The stories are endless. I once heard a middle-aged man say in reference to his wife, "I don't try to understand her. I just do what she says and give her what she wants, and this makes for a happier home!" Humorously told, he apparently holds a similar view to many married men I have encountered in the past. This notion also gives modern-day credence to the enormous impact of women in families and their role in creating domestic bliss. In Proverbs 21:9 we read, "It is better to dwell in a corner of the housetop than with a brawling woman in a wide house!" Wisdom speaks volumes in the passage Proverbs 14:1: "The wise woman builds her house, but with her own hands the foolish one tears hers down."

Modern-day translation: "If Momma isn't happy, no one is happy!" This statement alludes to the transient state of womanhood and that through self-evaluation, married women too must continue to reconcile their attitudes, beliefs, and actions toward circumstances. Evidence that women need to employ self-evaluation strategy comes supported by testimonials from those closest to them. Ask family members and friends how they think you have been handling your singlehood, with grace or with defiance. Brace yourself for the truth. You will surely need it.

Who Can Set the Example?

Honestly, most single women are flooded with so many idealist messages on relationships that it is difficult for them to parse fact from fiction; that is, what is real for one may be entirely impractical for another. From media images to strictly prescribed religious doctrine inundated with standards for living, the lives of single women can resemble dashboard-top bobble-head dolls—up and down and around, until things settle, or she comes to a sudden unpleasant jolt. It is then that she discovered things were completely out of control long ago.

Gleaning relationship advice from Carrie Bradshaw, the sassily clad character from Sex and the City, the wildly popular television series and motion picture sequel, no longer suffices as a model of the single life. Women are searching for something more. Have you ever wondered why Carrie pursued her inaccessible love interest, Mr. Big, with such tenacity, despite his preoccupation with making Carrie feel so small? Her monologue voiceovers detailed unimaginable accounts of Mr. Big's betrayal, emotional insensitivity, and blatant disregard for fidelity in relationships. We will not pick on "Big," as he is so affectionately called. After all, love and respect are real, and behaviors allowed become behaviors perpetuated. It would serve viewers well to notice the cyclical pattern that exists between Carrie and "Big": kiss, fight, flight, and make up. This pattern then repeated itself; remember the bobble-head-doll motif?

What gives? I agree that Mr. Big was a one amazing fellow. He was successful, handsome, an all-out alpha male as society defines it.

My view is this: "Big" had enormous capacity to express and receive love. He just needed someone to create this standard of expectation. After all, when the bar is set very low regarding love and respect, men give only what is required. Ladies, this is true. Some men may even consider dinner and a movie sufficient exchange for putting in the real work of getting to know you personally. The rationale is why do more when she has already agreed to date me formally before really knowing her? Then, that is all; dinner and a movie become the perceived expectation. This makes sense, and so does evaluating your current relationship expectation and aligning your views with principles of wholeness, purity, and self-respect.

Raise the bar; up the standard! Meeting someone should enhance you, not confuse you. It is simply too confusing to spend time dating someone who does not uphold standards you so dearly value. Ladies, talk first—spend time finding out the critical details before formal dating. Once you entangle yourself in a less-than-adequate dating arrangement, it then becomes difficult to see things for what they really are. Dim lights, toothy smiling, and profuse complimenting can be pleasantly distracting, but nonetheless a distraction from discovering the truth sooner instead of later. Seek the truth first. Take off the blinders. You are worth it; you deserve the best.

Secular themes for single women in dating relationships are not the only conundrums, but so are some well-meaning faith and values-based messages from singles' networks, community groups, and ministries. They are sometimes outdated and somewhat unrealistic. Yes, I said it. Can we get something from the twenty-first century, folks?

The upstanding single woman often finds herself asking, "Is there a place for modern women of integrity in the church?" I'll illustrate my point. I attended a reputable local ministry whose congregational theme was "we are a two-parent ministry." Huh? That was my exact sentiment. Well-intended, I am sure; however, this statement could have easily been interpreted as one that excludes singles and celebrates married people only. Didn't they know that over half the US population is single?

It is noble to celebrate marriage—God ordained it—but certainly not at the expense of polarizing singlehood. Single women are valuable. I should have hung around for an explanation.

Authentic Authority

Unlike secular views, true alpha men reproduce themselves in others by employing legitimate authority and authentic leadership skills. Legitimate authority (or what results from using ethical leadership strategies) always gives advantage to others. On the other hand, illegitimate authority uses manipulative charisma to forge connections with others for self-serving goals only. In other words, powerful alpha men identify as such because they invest time developing others, helping others reach their goals. In turn, authority exchanges from leader to follower in the form of an action. True leaders always have a dedicated following.

Furthermore, people become interested in what the alpha man has to say because he has invested so much time in them already. It is never difficult to join forces with an alpha. Accomplishing shared goals with an alpha is easy; people grow personally from merely being in his presence. After all, alphas take the role of mentor with unassuming fervor.

Wise Leadership

The alpha man is a wise or prudent leader. You may have heard the notion, "If you want to know how good a leader is, just go ask the followers." As the saying goes, the proof of the pudding is in the eating. Ongoing self-development forms the foundation from which alphas draw shared wisdom. Alphas live to share what life has taught them! It is typical for them to rally, with little effort, a band of wide-eyed protégées for any task or just because they very much like being in the company of alphas.

Remember this: alphas love to reproduce themselves. This process need not be a formal one. Over the years, I have encountered many young men who spend their weekends mentoring teens. Some volunteer at their local community center. It can begin here.

The best example I have encountered to illustrate this principle is through the servant-leadership model. Few can embrace the tenets of servant leaders better than John Maxwell, and in his book Becoming a Person of Influence, we see what it takes to influence people: "To become a person of influence, you have to love people before you try to lead them. The moment that people know that you care for and about them, the way they feel about you changes."

Alphas do not embrace this notion as superficial principle by which ten-step formulae apply to get a desired result, but rather first consider themselves people developers and character builders. This is their only noble duty, one to which many can take a grab, but only one can complete the part of the equation God had intended. Alphas love a challenge! Alphas love serving and leading people.

What Does the Alpha Man Look Like?

Every man has alpha potential. Likewise, by virtue of creation, single women may also discover where they fit as an alpha (see chapter 9: "Pot 'o'

Gold"). Women also will discover what questions to ask a man to uncover which character traits define his "alpha mechanics" aptitude.

1. Integrity:Does he buckle under pressure to do the right thing?
2. Purity:Does he reflect pure thoughts and have sincere actions toward you?
3. Strength:Does he make tough calls, even if he does not benefit personally?
4. Leadership: Is he passive or does he prefer that you take the lead in the relationship?
5. Courage: Does his life and occupation show evidence of responsible risk taking?

ALPHA WOMEN AND DATING

Just "Friends"

Cherish covenant friendships with single males. Even if he is not the person you will ultimately marry, it is still all right to admire him. I cannot stress enough the importance of this point. Women in preparation will glean from their male friends the character strengths and even personality traits considered most desirable and compatible with their own. Single women might also learn areas of strength and weakness in their own lives regarding relationships in general.

I have found interactions like these provide excellent personal growth opportunities for both sexes when in its purest form, without contamination from commitment expectations. I have experienced personally the mutual benefits of befriending single men as covenant friends. I know some of the brightest eligible bachelors around! They are my friends only. They have served as key supporters in my periods of growth, and I in theirs. We read in Proverbs 27:17, "As iron sharpens iron, so one man sharpens another." Let's face it: women relate to other women quite differently; friendships with other women are foundational and have theirs place. Men can add, however, a unique, well-rounded relationship perspective.

I Like You Too, But …

Motives for befriending a single man should not be commitment driven. Unless there is confirmed mutual interest outside of friendship only, err on the side of caution before spending extensive time with or making emotional investment in a single man who has not yet agreed to be a part of and lead a relationship with you. Friends are friends, and sizing up a potential mate is another thing altogether. Single women will be surprised to learn that some men, with whom they spend a lot of time, have no idea that she and he are an item or that she has interest beyond friendship. Okay, let us say in concert, duh! Men simply do not think about relationships as women do. This is true. He likes you, and you like him, but beyond mere admiration, there should be no assumptions. I stress mutual interest because unless a single man has verbalized his intention for a relationship by expressing his intentions to you personally and perhaps publicly among a few close friends, assume nothing more than casual friendship.

Playing the Game

Relationships are not really like games. Honestly, I am uncomfortable with this comparison, but I realize some truths we might gather from it. For example, I was reminded once by a male friend that "interacting with men is like playing chess or poker." Not being one for relationship rules of thumb, I sided partially with this game-relationship motif, snickered at his comment, and awaited a thorough explanation. I had hoped it would be a good one. It was. I became quite surprised to see value in a metaphor he had conjured up in sixty seconds flat. The logic was simple: the ability to size up another game player is as essential as having skills mastery for the game itself. Quick moves bring on rapid follow-up moves.

What's the point here? Somewhat in jest, I think my friend's point was this: bluffing and entertaining displays of gamesmanship are merely parts of the game culture that few take too seriously. It is unwise to place high value on decisions made on verbal cues only or on the perceived intent of another player. Along with sizing up a player too soon, use caution before reacting to diverting facial expressions and directional comments, although they may seem to give away someone's intent.

Refuse to be passive in your evaluation. Consider these merely fluff until "cards toss, pieces move."

In other words, in dating relationships, assume noting until he makes a move first, by verbal affirmation and action. Likewise, single women should caution themselves before giving away their hearts through their mouths! In other words, be careful not reveal too much too soon. True men of God enjoy the process of getting to know you in a predictable way. Telling your life story in the first two conversations is, shall we say, way too much. Likewise, discussing your intent to marry in the next two years is quite off-putting unless the gent has expressed similar interest first. Listen closely to his conversation, and match yours accordingly. If he is taking you on a fast ride that you are unwilling to take, remember to set boundaries and put on the brakes! Pacing your interaction with a man reveals the kind of maturity he will come to respect in the end. Likewise, paced interaction can reveal when to end distracting interactions going nowhere.

Most single women can relate to what happens when rushing things because they too have experienced disappointment and hurt from unfulfilled relationship expectations. Disappointment is no doubt inevitable in any relationship. However, learning to ask the right questions at the right time can serve to pad hearts for unexpected jolts from revealed truths. Unmistakably, a single man is capable of clearly stating what he intends; if he does not, it is best to assume casual friendship only. Single women, it would serve you well to govern your behaviors accordingly. Keep your high standards. Be accountable to another mature person. Let wisdom guide all interactions; ask her for help if you need it. In Proverbs 4:6, we read, "Do not forsake wisdom, and she will protect you; love her, and she will watch over you." Brutal honesty now prevents deep disappointment and time lost to emotional recovery later.

Building a Foundation

With great wisdom, single women responsibly ensure the momentum, integrity, or strength of a relationship; on the other hand, single men determine its timing and direction. In other words, strong relationships are not relationships of emotional, physical, and financial compromise. Likewise, strong relationships exist because of deep, well-constructed foundations, and building them requires deliberation and proper timing.

To illustrate my point: Imagine pouring concrete in the morning; allowing it to cure by midafternoon, and the next day begin constructing a new home. What a disaster! Most people know it can take up to a week for concrete to cure. What is interesting? Concrete looks house-ready well before this time, but building too soon will surely uncover foundational cracks. Foundational cracks lower property values. Are you setting the proper foundation for your future relationships? Do you know your true value? We read in Proverbs 31:10, you are more "precious than rubies"!

CASE STUDY: WE'RE GETTING MARRIED

Perhaps for single women I only assumed the entire who-I'm-going to marry motif is exhausting. The truth is this: women actually enjoy anticipating this event. You know, just like Cinderella. Women love romance, fairy tales, and the idea that there is a special someone out there searching for them—that is, if the shoe fits. For the sake of good storytelling, chronicling how a woman eventfully meets "the one" God intended for her has an unmistakable flair of mysticism to it. I love my sister friends, hearing their romantic interludes with all the Mr. "Almost-the-Ones," and finally, celebrating the news of their impending God-ordained unions in marriage to "The One" really.

This leads me to retell the story my friend Topya shared with me. "Our first kiss will be at the altar!" she belted and then exhaled in sheer amazement with the ideal herself. Topya will be marrying in two months, after a yearlong courtship and a four-month engagement. We met through a mutual male friend she was seeing at the time. It is funny how things work out this way. She will not marry the friend of mine but an amazing young evangelist from Colorado. He saw her image in a dream, and what a picture of perfection he saw! Topya is simply beautiful, and her physical beauty pales in comparison to the finely tempered womanly character she possesses. She is such an asset and perfectly suited to support her future husband in ministry. Naturally, he is very capable of encouraging her in ministry pursuits. Toypa's fiancé knew she was "the one"; he claims to have seen a vision of her. Other key details confirmed his belief. He knew her when he saw her. How cool was that!

Divine Connection

Topya's story reminds me of the biblical account of Isaac and Rebekah. Abraham, the "father of many nations," sought the wife God had intended for his son, Isaac. This was no ordinary pursuit; let's not think any women for Abraham's son would suffice. Abraham took seriously the power of spiritual inheritance and his role as patriarch of Israel, one who responsibly ensured God's will operated the progeny of God's chosen people. Abraham pursued the will of God for his life, and naturally, divine providence affected his entire family. Therefore, with specific instruction, Abraham's servant traveled to the land of Abraham's relatives in search of a bride for his son, Isaac. In Genesis 24:43–44, we read the servant's account of Abraham's instructions:

> See, I am standing here beside this spring. This is my request. When a young woman comes to draw water, I will say to her, "Please give me a little drink of water from your jug." If she says, "Yes, have a drink, and I will draw water for your camels too," let her be the one you have selected to be the wife of my master's son.

Assured this trip would be effortless, he carefully followed Abraham's instructions, as an angel guided his journey. It all happened as Abraham instructed his servant: Rebekah offered the servant and his camel water and a place to retire from the long journey. This was the very act signaling the servant that Rebekah, the woman at the fountain, was Isaac's future wife!

True to form, the initial meeting between Toypa and her fiancé came through a mature church member whom, through another young woman, Topya had befriended. Funny thing is, Topya's future husband was the love interest of this young woman, and at the time, Toypa had no idea to which young man the young woman was referring. As it turns out, neither did Topya's future husband! Imagine that. Women frequently target fanciful "marry me" radar toward the most eligible Christian bachelors. The thing is, these young men rarely know them! Do not get me wrong. I believe some women do know beforehand who their potential suitor might be. However, chances of this happening are slim to none without a first meeting. I know, most unions do not come together as such destined meetings. Playing out just like in the Bible or a fantastic movie does make this story quite intriguing, and while few will have the same one to tell, I feel we all should believe in God-ordained marriage. Keep hoping for yours too.

Let's Get Physical—Wait!

Talk of physical intimacy before marriage is common among Christian singles. The Bible is clear here: flee fornication (1 Corinthians 6:18). And for good reason, avoiding lip-locking until marriage is a doable, admirable feat, though it's certainly not easy for most dating couples.

The point is clear. Upholding a standard of purity speaks to the value couples place on integrity in dating relationships. We can glean much from this example. Without having to ask, I gather that couples can create more time to learn about each other's interests in a manner unclouded by emotional charges brought on by physical intimacy. Simple attraction involves enough oomph to charge any romantic interaction; anything more than this is overwhelming and hinders authentic exchange between two people who genuinely like each other. Learning about each other takes real work. Evaluating compatibility, working through prospective personality quirks, and staging methods for conflict resolution set a solid foundation for growth in any relationship.

THE CHALLENGE

For many single women, things have not worked out very well in the past. Consider this not an unfortunate life sentence but rather an excellent opportunity to begin anew! Another truth is that not all single women will marry. Some may question whether our purpose begins after marriage. The answer is no. There lies a future full of reasons to embrace life assertively, in a manner consistent with God's purpose for your life, which began before you were born. Accept the challenge to seek purpose in all interactions. You can begin by evaluating the reasons you ultimately pursue interactions with others. Is it to gain something you need? To win approval from someone whom you admire? Do you even know why? Undoubtedly, you will involve yourself in many casual meetings; however, single women of purpose seek out the most meaningful, mutually beneficial relationships. For the purposefully single, few and far between are there fruitless encounters, associations, or relationships.

Seek Completion First

Filling your "God space": We all feel emptiness at times and await the chance to connect with others, hoping to fill a companionship void. After realizing that we require more than what another can humanly provide to fill our longings, we become very disappointed. People are not to blame; they simply cannot satisfy the yearning we have in our hearts for God. By design, it rarely works out in a manner that fully satisfies our need for divine connection. Employing other methods to get our emotional needs met only short-sights our road to wholeness, what we experience as an offering from God just for asking Him to fill our empty places. Work to fill your "God space." As your Creator, God is ultimately your first desire, even if you fail to realize this at first. He designed it this way.

Get the Right Perspective

Much of what causes angst for the purposefully single resolves itself with the right perspective. Get the right perspective. Get it now! Nothing seems to help balance perspectives as well as consulting God regarding your interactions with others. Seek to grow personally, in relationship with Him, while you grow with those who are within your sphere of influence. No one can fill the place that relationship with God can. I have found it fascinating, the way single women describe what it is like when their time with God goes lacking because of life obligations. We can all relate to this.

GOD: MY FIRST LOVE

Have you ever been wooed by the spirit of God? God is your eternal knight in shining armor, your first love! He has no need to compete with other loves, since He has pierced your heart to long for Him first. God waits patiently for you to give Him His due time with you. He makes this experience so unforgettable that you will not be able to resist Him, so in quietness and sometimes in secret, you'll prepare for His arrival, over and over again.

Make spending time with God your priority. Go ahead and do it! Fill a special room with scented candles; program your iPod with your favorite worship songs. Set the mood with a mind-set of expectation. That's right; you are creating an environment to get to know someone. Will you prepare for Him properly? Do not be shy. Since it's common for single women to go out of their way to impress a potential suitor, why not give God the same treatment? He will surely receive you without reservation. You will not have to guess His motives; He loves you already. You will not have to wonder about His intentions. Know that He intends to make His time with you so special, you will want to keep it secret but cannot. The joy you will experience in His presence will be contagious. You'll want to share this experience with those you encounter.

CONFESSION FOR THE PURPOSEFULLY SINGLE WOMAN

As a single woman, I will not prepare for the marriage event only. Instead, I will prepare for You, Lord, by first cultivating a relationship with You. In deep intimacy with You, I will discover keys to becoming a successful daughter, sister, friend, wife, mother, and good steward of all things You have given me. From these keys, I will unlock strength of character, practice integrity in all my affairs, master my emotions, and learn to celebrate my successes and the successes of other women. I will practice purity of thought and purity in all my actions; commit to ongoing self-discovery; evaluate my areas of weakness and work to perfect them according to Your standards. If I am to marry, all these things will be attractive to my future mate. I will draw him not with crafty womanliness, trickery, or manipulation, but out of a pure spirit. My spirit will draw him; my attractiveness will pique his interest in me. One day, our paths will cross; he will be watching me, and then he will make himself known at the right time. Until then, and always, I hid myself in You, perfecting all things concerning You, Lord. I trust you, Father, believing that your timing is always perfect. Amen.

BIBLIOGRAPHY

Blue Letter Bible. "The Purpose of God." Accessed March 17, 2010. www. blueletterbible.com.

"KJV Concordance for 'Integrity.'" Accessed November 19, 2009. http:// www.blueletterbible.org/search/translationResults.cfm?Criteria= integrity&t=KJV.

Brainyquote. "Joseph Campbell Qui." March 2009. http://www. brainyquote.com/quotes/quotes/j/josephcamp386014.html.

Cathy, S. Truett. 1989. It's Easier to Succeed Than to Fail. Hampton, VA: Thomas Nelson, Inc.

Donin, Hayim Halevy. 1972. To Be a Jew: A Guide to Jewish Observance in Contemporary Life. New York: Basic Books.

Edwards, Ieasha. 2010. The Potter's Refinement Project. Atlanta, GA: Unpublished.

Google Books. "Pocket Dictionary of Ethics." Stanley J. Grenz and Jay T. Smith. Accessed November 18, 2009. http://books.google.com/ books?id=2dLuym2H4PQC.

Merriam-Webster Dictionary for "Glean". Accessed November 25, 2010. https://www.merriam-webster.com/dictionary/glean

Monroe, Miles. 2004. Rediscovering the Kingdom. Shippensburg, PA: Destiny Image Publishers.

Moore, Beth. 2008. "Esther: It's Tough Being a Woman." Nashville, TN: Lifeway Church Resources, Video Session 1.

Rowling, J. K. Harry Potter and the Sorcerer's Stone. London: Bloomsbury Children's, 1997.

Torrey, R. A. 2005. Presence and Work of the Holy Spirit. New Kensington, PA: Whitaker House Publishers.

Whitta, Gary. The Book of Eli (film). Sony Pictures/Warner Brothers. 2010.

Wikipedia contributors. "Bayer designation." Wikipedia, The Free Encyclopedia. Wikipedia, The Free Encyclopedia, 10 Sep. 2017. Web. 11 Apr. 2018.

Wikipedia contributors. "Alpha ethnology." Wikipedia, The Free Encyclopedia. Wikipedia, The Free Encyclopedia, 7 Apr. 2018. Web. 11 Apr. 2018.

Wikipedia contributors. "Alpha and beta carbon." Wikipedia, The Free Encyclopedia.

Wikipedia, The Free Encyclopedia, 4 Apr. 2018. Web. 11 Apr. 2018. Wikipedia contributors. "Terms alpha." Wikipedia, The Free Encyclopedia. Wikipedia, The Free Encyclopedia, 26 Feb. 2018. Web. 3 Mar. 2018.

Wikipedia contributors. "Q-learning." Wikipedia, The Free Encyclopedia. Wikipedia, The Free Encyclopedia, 11 Apr. 2018. Web. 11 Apr. 2018.

Wikipedia contributors. "Whole tone scale." Wikipedia, The Free Encyclopedia. Wikipedia, The Free Encyclopedia, 11 Apr. 2018. Web. 11 Apr. 2018.

www.ingramcontent.com/pod-product-compliance
Lightning Source LLC
Chambersburg PA
CBHW021653120626
46545CB00002B/840